THEN

&

NOW

SIMON GRIEVES

A catalogue record for this book is available from the National Library of Australia

Copyright © 2023 Simon Grieves
All rights reserved.
ISBN: 978-1-922727-68-8

Linellen Press
265 Boomerang Road
Oldbury, Western Australia
www.linellenpress.com.au

Contents

Contents iii
Preface 1
Dedication 3
   The Policeman's Poem 5
Chapter 1 - What's in a Name? 11
   Bashed *15*
   Runover *31*
   'Fragged' *34*
Chapter 2 - Hostage Rescue 43
Chapter 3 - Suicide by Cop 51
Chapter 4 - Mongrel Dog 58
Chapter 5 - Officer Down 63
Chapter 6 - The Informer 68
Chapter 7- Camp Crusty 73
Chapter 8 - The Job's Fucked 87
Chapter 9- Claremont Serial Killer 93
Chapter 10 - Olympic Flame 94
Chapter 11 - The Good Times 100
   Dining-In Night *107*
Chapter 12 - IRAQ 112
Chapter 13 - Guinea 133

Chapter 14 - Ring of Fire 152
Chapter 15 - Indonesia 157
   VALE. Hemi Williams *170*
Chapter 16 - Manus Island 171
Chapter 17- Tanzania 186
Chapter 18 - Frequent Flyers 204
Chapter 19 - Blue Blood 220

Preface

I am proud to have worn the blue uniform: I served eighteen years in the Western Australia Police Force and now as a security consultant working around the world. This book is a 'warts and all', call-it-as-I-see-it insight into working as an operator in the Western Australian Police counter-terrorism unit, the Tactical Response Group – *Then* – and as a private security contractor – *Now*. I have written about some of the more memorable incidents and the black humour, which makes our kind tick. I recount my time from policing the streets of the city, to running 'Route Irish' in Baghdad, to chasing illegal miners deep down underground in the mines of Africa, my life, threatened several times and not always coming out the other side unscathed, injured during training in the 'Kill House', run over, bashed unconscious, to staring down the barrel of a gun, not once but twice. It is not about slagging off anyone, just an expression of opinion based on personal experience from my own perspective.

You may agree to disagree with me on my views – that is your prerogative – but allow me to also have my own.

This book gives a raw and honest insight into the character of the people who do the kind of work we do. Politically incorrect, my opinion sometimes confronting, the language colourful, but it is all true and very real. For that, I make no apology. If you are squeamish or a PC type, you have been warned. Enjoy.

Simon Grieves (aka 'BLOCK')

Dedication

I always said that one day I would write a book and I guess many of us have said that at some time in our lives – to write a book about your experiences, thoughts, and opinions or simply to express yourself. I never seemed to have the time or the inclination to put pen to paper ... that was until I found myself in one of the most difficult periods in my life, not one that I could use my skills to defeat or rely on my raw determination to overcome.

In the first half of 2014, my dad was diagnosed with pancreatic and liver cancer, terminal. Right at that time I was forced to take an unwanted hiatus from a contract which turned out to be a blessing in disguise, and I was able to look after my dad to the end.

In the ensuing months of my dad's treatment, I spent as much time as I could with him – I guess I was trying to make up for the time I had lost with him from working around the world and dedicating myself to the Police Force – visiting him at home in the mornings; taking him for his chemotherapy treatment; visiting him again in the evenings; picking him up off the bathroom floor when he was too sick and weak from the chemo, his body slowly withering away until eventually, he had to move into palliative care where I watched him slowly become physically half the man he used to be, waste away and die.

At this point, I would like to express my sincerest thanks and utmost respect to the palliative care nurses who looked after him and made sure he did not suffer and that he died with dignity, if cancer will allow you to do that.

Returning home in the evenings, I found myself struggling to come to grips with it all. I had seen dead bodies at crime scenes, the carnage of war and poverty around the world. But this was different. I had the support of my family, for which I am eternally thankful. They have had to put up with all my shit over the years – the shift work; not coming home, and not knowing what I was doing, or where, and sometimes finding out on the evening news; spending months away from home; not being there for key moments in their lives – graduations, birthdays and anniversaries – me always wanting to sit facing the door at restaurants; places where I could not take my family in order to keep them safe from the low-lifes I had locked up over the years.

But what I am experiencing now is very different. I am hurting deep inside. So, late at night when everyone has gone to bed, I am left with my thoughts and to ponder life, such that it is, and I could not find the answer at the bottom of a glass of single malt. So, I put pen to paper and wrote this book and in doing so found it to be cathartic and make sense where sense could be made.

Unfortunately, I didn't get to finish the first draft before Dad passed away and went to be with his maker. I would have dearly loved for him to have been able to be the first one to read it. In a strange turn of events, it was his illness that found me writing this book, and in his death, finishing it. I would like to dedicate this book in loving memory, and in honour of, my dad.

RIP Dad. I love you.

Robert Stuart Grieves
Born January 8th, 1936.
Died August 3rd, 2014.

The Policeman's Poem

*I have been where you fear to be
I have seen what you fear to see
I have done what you fear to do,
All these things I have done for you.
I am the one you lean upon,
The one you cast your scorn upon,
The one you bring your troubles to,
All these things I have been for you.
The one you ask to stand apart,
The one you feel should have no heart,
The one you call the 'man in blue'
But I am a person, just like you.
And when you watch a person die,
And hear a battered baby cry,
Then do you think that you can be
All these things you ask of me?*

*And through the years,
I have come to see,
That I am not what you ask of me.
So, take this badge, take this gun,
Will you take it,
Will anyone?*

The preceding poem pretty much sums up how I feel about a job I love but can no longer do to the best of my ability. I have dealt with what can only be described as the animals of our society: the rapists, paedophiles, murderers, and drug dealers peddling their poison to the vulnerable and weak; coming to trust no one, damned if I did and damned if I didn't – the only person I trust is myself – to be assaulted by the very people I had sworn to protect, and to witness the pitiful punishment meted out by our criminal justice system. And that is exactly what it is: justice for the criminal. No justice for the victims, their families, or meeting the expectations of the wider community; offering no punishment or deterrent to the crim, or future crims. A Police Force rebranded as a 'Service', administered by out-of-touch academic boffins with political aspirations, the presumption of innocence not afforded to its own officers and further insult added to injury by keyboard warriors, the media, and politicians criticising, judging and demonising you at every opportunity.

It seemed that locking up crooks was no longer the objective of policing. Police protect the innocent, vulnerable and weak. Not to be psychologists, drug counsellors, doctors and marriage guidance officers.

Getting a foot in the door in the local security industry frustrated by an industry plagued with inept regulation, incestuous relations, wannabes and wankers, life as a Private Security Contractor (PSC) is not smooth going either. I gave it a good go though, before I realised my efforts were, in the most part, futile, and so eventually enough was enough. I hit the 'circuit' as they call it in the trade: I became a private security contractor, or as some call us, a mercenary.

I will clarify: A mercenary is a soldier of fortune, a person who will work for anyone who will pay. The likes of war lords, illegitimate regimes and crime czars. Private security contractors are by the most, disciplined, contracted individuals from military special forces or police tactical units and accountable to a government authority or a government-contracted employer, observing international norms and rule of law.

THEN

Chapter 1

What's in a Name?

I am in deepest darkest Africa. I know, I know, you're thinking steaming jungle, buzzing biting insects and the sounds of an exotic bird calling from the green canopy above. Indiana Jones stuff, right? Well not quite. I'm sitting in a rusted ore cart, about the size of a bucket on a skid steer, stuck halfway down a 900m near-vertical mine shaft in Tanzania, wondering *what the fuck I am doing here?* Well, I did say it was in deepest darkest Africa. C'mon, would I lie to you? I used to be a Policeman!

The air is thick and has a warm humid smell about it, just like when you can tell first thing in the morning that it's going to be a stinker (hot) of a day. Eerily quiet, broken only by the steel cable creaking under the strain of me sitting in the ore cart and with just enough headroom to look out over the top of the cart to see daylight the size of a 5-cent piece as my beacon to the top. I ask myself, *What the fuck am I doing here? Block, you have to write a book one day.* And here it is.

I will get back to Tanzania, but first let me expand on who is 'Block'. Everyone has a nickname. Your mum and dad will have one for you, a pet name, your 'life partner' – *Fuck me, this politically correct (PC) thing has gotten ridiculous* – and your mates will give you a nickname. It will be for various reasons: how you look, behave, something you do, something unique about you, some flattering and some not so flattering, as is normally the case when everyone takes the piss at the soonest opportunity and more so in my line of work. Guys earn their nicknames through physical prowess or feats of human endurance they had performed in the field (and off) or for a particular personal characteristic or trait. Typically, you have your 'Ranga' or 'Blue' but there are more apt or descriptive nicknames. There's Ned, a born-again Christian (from the TV show *The Simpsons*) and Horse (and trust me he was hung like one – or at least he was ... ... but that's another story for another time). The following events are however to earn me my nickname. 'Blocker', 'Blockhead' and eventually just simply, 'Block'. Granted I had a head start (no pun intended), but I do have a head like a smashed crab. As they say, 'only the face a mother could love'. *Bastards.*

I was a cop for eighteen years, of which I spent about seven years in GDs (General Duties), five years as a weapons instructor at the police academy and six years at the Counter Terrorism Unit, the Tactical Response Group or more commonly known as the 'TRG'. I consider myself an average operator, a reasonable shot with the pistol, half reasonable with a rifle. No superstar and definitely there are guys who are born naturals on the tools and can shoot the dick off a bee 100 feet away. Me, I had to work hard at everything, learning from my mistakes as I went, and I made a few, for which I served my penance.

I am an average bloke who grew up in Port Hedland in the northwest of Western Australia; no Rhodes scholar and I quit high school at the end of first term in Year 12, having passed not one exam. Sorry ... yes, I did pass one if a 50% score is a pass. Having visions of grandeur about joining the navy or air force as a pilot (*dream on*) at one stage, I ended up working at the Oyster Beds seafood restaurant down in East Fremantle as a dishwasher for a while and sharing a flat in Como with two high school mates who had also moved to the big smoke from the 'Nor West'. Both were studying at Uni while I also did a stint in a fruit and veg shop before I had an epiphany and decided to join the Police Force.

I was nineteen, joining on November 29, 1982 and graduating on my twentieth birthday. I grew up quickly in the cops. I had to. My parents had also moved back to Perth and I moved in and out of home a couple of times during the academy, the relationship with my parents, or Mum to be more precise, was strained at times and Dad went with the flow to keep the peace and make his own life easier, no doubt. I eventually ended up sharing a flat near the academy where some other recruits were living. What a shit hole! And we all moved out when we quickly grew tired of our delightful neighbours constantly knocking on the door asking for help when their de-facto had come home drunk, again, or abusing us for being 'Copper Cunts' or hitting one of us up for $20 or some smokes. *Nice*. And I was only a baggy-arsed recruit. What was it going to be like when I became a 'real cop'?

I have an older brother who is nothing like me. Not in looks, interests, politics, music, nothing. I tried once or twice to have a brotherly relationship with him but it was just too hard; too much time had passed, as had water under the bridge, my relationship, or lack thereof with my brother, vindicated when the prick wouldn't come to his own father's funeral when Dad passed away. I guess whatever demons there were between my dad and brother were still there, and not been buried. So, I learnt to be independent fairly early in life, no choice really, but I grew up respecting the cops as Dad had a few mates who were cops when we lived in Port Hedland and I got to meet a few. I guess they left an impression on me that I did not realise at the time.

There's some interesting history as it turns out about my family tree. My great-grandfather had been, in his time, the tallest Police Officer in the London Met, standing 6 foot 11 inches or something, so I guess it was in my blood to start with.

So how did an average bloke like me get into an elite Police counter-terrorism unit like the TRG? Firstly, I am determined, driven to a point of being stubborn; dedicated to whatever I turn my hand to. All in or nothing at all. I am proud to have been a Police Officer and proud to have served my community but, in the latter years of my career, the job became something else which I could not relate with. So, whilst I was still young enough and at what I considered the pinnacle of my career – a member of the TRG – I decided to resign.

I ran a fairly successful security training business for twelve years or so after I left 'The Job', (as we cops call it), and entered the world of private security where I am today.

So how did I earn my nickname 'Block'. Who is Block?

Bashed

It is 1989. The internet has not come of age, so social media like Facebook is not around and mobile phones are still out of reach of the average school kid, thankfully, otherwise who knows how this night could have turned out. But the young ones are pretty adept to spreading the word and by word of mouth and flyers sent out inviting anyone and everyone to a 'House Wrecking Party' – it's a party destined to turn to shit from the start.

Located in an upmarket coastal suburb where the 'Real Housewives' of Perth live, the coiffured of society, 'Dinks' dressed by Alex Perry and Carla Zampatti (you know the type) gaze out across the Indian Ocean to Rottnest Island from their second-floor balcony sipping from champagne flutes, little finger cocked, and just down the side streets are the original surviving beach houses now rented by the 'Grommets' whose only care in life is catching the next set of waves. I can remember, as a kid, when we lived in Perth, Dad would drive us in his HR Holden wagon, for what seemed like hours, to this very beachside suburb along limestone tracks to reach the coast and ride the huge surf on an old tractor tyre inner tube. There was no housing around back then.

On this night, an old fibro weatherboard beach shack is earmarked for demolition, the mung beans evicted to make way for another mansion to compete for the million-dollar views on the west coast and the blue of the Indian Ocean. The party is in full swing, a live band, eighteen beer kegs on tap and about 700 boozed-up pubescent teenagers running amuck. What better reason than to hold a 'House Wrecking Party'.

Combine that with a little entrepreneurship, that is, charge an entry fee to cover the grog and band and maybe make some money on the side with which to buy the next bag of mull (cannabis) and you have yourself a recipe for disaster.

The L&G (Liquor & Gaming Enforcement) guys are in attendance due to the illegal sale of alcohol, supplying underage drinkers, no liquor license permit and so on. A request from VKI (Police Communications) for a uniform presence goes out over the Police radio net to provide assistance. L&G guys work in civvy's (street wear) so they can go into the bars and clubs unnoticed (supposedly) but when you don't line up in the queue along with everybody else waiting to get into the nightclub and generally not pay for your drinks, everyone knows they are cops anyway. When we (the TRG) aren't kicking in doors we are usually in uniform.

On this night, we just happen to be down the road at the Hillary's boat harbour, so I put our hand up for Oscar Five (our call sign) to attend. On arriving, effectively, it appears there is only three uniform cops present. You do the math: there is not much we can do so I call for backup and we wait. In the meantime, there are kids smoking dope, couples going at it like rabbits on the front lawns of neighbouring gardens while others are punching on fuelled by the excess of booze, and we just have to stand there and let it happen, powerless to stop it while we cop the barrage of verbal abuse from the sweet little darlings. The atmosphere is palpable.

The L&G want to shut the party down and we have no police vans to lock anyone up in. The merits of shutting the party down are discussed with a L&G Sergeant and I suggest, 'At least let's get some reinforcements here before they do shut it down'. And so it was agreed, or so I thought. But fuck me dead, within five minutes or so, someone in their infinite wisdom does the reverse and shuts the party down. The kegs are pulled and the unmistakable sound of gas venting as the tap spears are pulled, accompanied by the band announcing the party is being shut down, is clearly not a popular move with the several hundred strong party goers. Hey, it isn't popular with me either.

The reaction is not good. We are met with boos and jeers from a now pissed off and charged up crowd. Our numbers have grown to about twenty or so when the bottles start to be hurled our way and things go pear-shaped really quick. So, it is to become known as the infamous 'Trigg Riot' and the first modern history riot in the state.

Our ranks grow, reinforcements arrive to bolster the numbers, the party organisers have taken prime position, sitting on the roof of the 'Love Shack', chanting "kill the pigs, kill the pigs." Then, just like you see on TV when the Palestinians stone the Israeli soldiers, missiles began raining down on us. We are totally outnumbered, and powerless, as mob mentality takes over on the streets and they attack. We stand back-to-back in a circle, flailing our batons, fending off drunken shitheads, all the while to the chant of "kill the pigs" by the cowards on the roof still egging them on. We need to regather our forces or face getting a serious flogging.

We seek the protection of our police vehicles. As a disciplined and trained team that is the TRG, we never 'Run Away', it's a 'Tactical Regroup', just as you are never lost, just 'Geographically Compromised'. A play on words maybe, but it is all about the positive mind set. I think it is this mental toughness that is the differentia between those who become members of the TRG and similar units around the world and those who do not. Even when physically and mentally buggered, and you can't think straight or put one foot in front of the other, you don't give up – never give up because you just never know that the next step forward is what it takes to win. I think it was my mental toughness and not so much my physical fitness that got me through the TRG selection course, and it was this that is to see me right on this particular night.

I have been in GD's (General Duties) for several years, posted to walking the beat in the city after graduating from the academy, then transferred to the port station of Fremantle where I spend a couple of years before picking up a spot at a local suburban station, when after a few more years, I decide to put in for selection to join the TRG. I guess I am finding GD's work a little boring, although I am having a blast, working in Fremantle during the America's Cup, 'Rotto' (Rottnest Island) on long weekends and brawls at the Raffles Hotel at closing time, which was always a good way to round off the week's afternoon shift before a week of long night shifts. My arrest rate is pretty good, and I've made some good 'pinches', but it is time to move on. If your application is accepted (which basically means you are not considered a cockhead, you get a tick next to your name and not a cross) you then do the preselection course which is based on the SASR (Special Air Service Regiment, or simply known as 'the Regiment') selection course condensed into a week of bastardry. Pass preselection and it is months of doing various weapons and tactics courses before you are considered at a level ready to go on jobs (effectively you are on probation until you pass all the courses) and accepted into the TRG permanently. Generally, it takes about five years before you're considered as an operator and can specialise if you wish (sniper, assaulter, water ops). Usually everyone excels at one particular skill set. For me, I guess it is as an 'Assaulter' or 'Door Kicker'.

TRG candidates are run ragged on the selection course. It makes sense when Perth is the home base for the SASR that the TRG has close links with the Regiment and there are a few former SASR and now TRG DS (Directional Staff) running my selection course. One such character (no names are mentioned to protect the innocent) is on my course. A short nuggetty fellow who had more flying time than Superman, more sea time than Neptune and more shooting time than the Lone Ranger, and what's more, he could back it. He had spent time seconded to the British 22SAS and was a Vietnam Vet. Much respect for this man amongst men, and now he is in the WA Police TRG as an Instructor and what he didn't know probably wasn't worth knowing. We'll call him Operator #1, who by the way, has picked up the filthy habit from his American SF (Special Forces) friends of chewing tobacco. He barks instructions at you and then spits out a wad of black tar. His gums and teeth stained from the sticky tobacco, it is perfect for this man's persona. I did try chewing tobacco once when offered by a Yank in Iraq – curiosity, I guess. I do enjoy a good cigar from time to time, so why not give it a try? You take a pinch of the sticky tar like tobacco out of the tin and then press it into and around your gums and teeth. The idea is that the nicotine is absorbed into the blood stream faster for the desired effect. Never again, my mouth, tongue and gums went numb with this tingling, stinging sensation and it tasted like shit. Operator #1 can keep it all to himself.

Operator #1 and the other DS put us through all sorts of physical and mental challenges designed to weed out the wannabes and wankers. You are pushed to your absolute limit of physical endurance. You ache all over; find muscles you never knew you had. Skin hangs from your feet from blisters that had burst, purple 'Mercurochrome' painted all over the soles of our feet to dry out the blisters. You take in your belt another notch as you drop yet another kilo from running for what seems like forever, and always fucking up hill, always hungry and always thirsty. And just when you think the day is over, you get given another 'Nav Ex' (Navigational Exercise) to complete and go stumbling through the bush trying to orientate map to ground and pick out features in the fading light.

Fuck, which way is north? Reminding myself that the sun rises in the east and sets in the west, I look in the direction between the sun setting on the horizon to my left, which must be west and the ensuing darkness to my right must be east, so straight ahead must be north and south is behind me, is my reasoning. I remember the basics the DS had taught us prior to the first 'Nav Ex' (Navigational Exercise). It helps when even the simplest of tasks become an embuggerance due to mental fatigue. For the week we are up at some ungodly hours when my body is usually climbing into bed, not out, only to be told to do things no one's body should be asked to do at any hour of the day and then to get choked half to death with tear gas, puking your guts up and then to have the meanest-looking, tattoo-covered, fittest, toughest SASR mother fucker PTI (Physical Training Instructor) yell his balls off at you in the gym at Swanbourne Barracks because you lose your grip on the climbing rope, ripping the callouses from the palms of your hands as you hopelessly try to stop your fall, feebly grabbing at the rope only to be described as 'Piss Weak' as you hit the mat below. Lying there with the wind knocked out of my lungs, I am fucked, every part of my body aches, and I have a sweat rash around my crotch and balls that's making me walk like I have shit myself. But I am not about to give in. I am not a quitter. Quitting is easy. I get up and have another crack at the rope. Certainly, I could be fitter and that would help. Other guys on selection seemed to be cruising. They were going to pass for sure.

I have made it to the end of the week and had not been dumped, yet. Guys had 'pulled the pin' (quit) on the course, some forced out by injury and others told to leave. It is the last day of selection. We started with a group of around twenty-five, and we are now down to at least half that. There is much speculation amongst those of us who are left about who is going to pass and who is not. Making it to the last day is still no guarantee. Even passing is no guarantee you will actually get picked up even when a vacancy exits and that's just the way it is and if you don't like it, well, stiff shit ... you aren't what they were looking for anyway.

Second last day and the DS put a BBQ and beers on, after yet another torturous day and we down the beers fast. I'm pissed after the first one as my body is running on empty. We are reassured that tomorrow, the last day, would be spent mostly cleaning kit and returning stores and then the boss of TRG would announce who had passed and that would be pretty much the day. I am elated to have made it this far, but it is still with some trepidation as to whether I would pass or even get a jersey.

It was a BBQ to remember, with DS#1 telling us war stories, all of us in awe of his exploits.

The next morning, not feeling the best as we had all had that one (or three) extra beers too many and, combined with the past week, late nights and early mornings (which were still night-time by my reckoning), I am suffering, but at least we are only going to be cleaning guns, returning equipment to the QM (Quarter Master), washing cars etc. Or so we think. *The lying bastards!*

As it turns out, it is another cunning plan of the DS to see how we are after a night on the piss, to see how we socialise as a group, who gets aggro, and how we pull up and perform after a late night. Just for something different, we are sent on a run, how unusual, but this time it's with a difference and the ambulance parked up nearby is a little unnerving. Still dressed in the overalls we had been wearing all week (I think I actually slept in mine that night), which now could stand up on their own on account of being salt encrusted by our sweat, snot and dirt (which is probably helping some of us stay upright as well), with our gas mask and pouch strapped around our leg, we are put into teams of four and told to stand next to a log. *Oh no, it's the infamous 'Log Run'. Fuck, I thought we had got away with not doing it. Oh, how wrong I am.*

When you decide to do the TRG selection course, you make it your business to find out as much as you can from those who had done it and if you're lucky, from a mate who is in TRG. That way you may be able to get some specific lead up training done if you lack in a particular area. But there really is no training for 'The Log Run' because you just cannot replicate the mental duress that accompanies this extreme physical test that can only be described as 'brutal'. And they had saved the best for last. These logs are actually cut down power poles of solid jarrah wood and they are heavy as shit. The log run is considered the catalyst of physical and mental testing and sorts the men from the boys.

As we run, the DS yells instructions at us.

"Above your heads, go."

The log is raised as high above our heads as our trembling arms will allow.

"On your backs, sit ups, go."

With the log across our chest, and arms hooked up under the log so it will not roll off, I don't know how many sit-ups we do, but every single one is punishing the abs and the bitumen road rubs our backs red raw.

"On your feet, let's go."

"Gas, gas, gas."

And with that we keep running – or whatever exercise they have us doing – and keep a hold of the log and put our gas mask on.

It's near on impossible, juggling the gas mask and the log in unison. And every now then one of the DS would single one of us out for special words of encouragement, like

"Give up now, you've failed anyway."

To compound the matter, we have a team mascot that must not be left unattended 24/7, be put on the ground, forgotten and shared equally among the teams. Our mascot was a solid clay brick, wrapped in hessian, hundred mile an hour tape and a piece of rope hanging off it, to help carry it, I guess. Doesn't sound much of a challenge I know, but the mascot is an embuggerance to everyone at some time or another during selection. The rationale behind this, what can only be described as torture, is to see who can work as a team and those who can't or won't. Fuck up the coordinated movement of the exercise and the team fails, dropping the log and yes, you guessed it, there are penalties if you do.

Donning our gas masks, we all sound like Darth Vader with a bad case of asthma, our breathing laboured as we try to force our sucking lungs to feed our oxygen-starved muscles to keep running and carrying the log that now feels like it weighs a ton. We have had to don our gas masks the previous day when exposed to tear gas in order to 'test our ability to follow directions and function whilst suffering the effects thereof', quote unquote. At least that is the justification we are given for what seems like such a cruel act. None of us have bothered to wash our gas masks as we simply just could not be arsed in the little spare time we had. Sleep was the priority. We are to suffer the consequences of our poor choice as we experience secondary contamination from the residue of the tear gas crystals on our masks and overalls.

When you're hot, sweating and gagging for air, tear gas is not your friend. Around the seal of my mask, my skin is burning, my eyes are stinging like shit and I have strands of snot running out of my nose. I just cannot suck in enough air through the filter of my gas mask. My lungs feel like they were about to collapse. But on we go, gas mask on, gas masks off, on, off, on, off. Then, one of the guys in a team in front of my team turns into a rag doll and goes down like a sack of shit and hits the road, 'he's fucked'. Now I know why the ambulance is on standby.

As we run past, the convulsing, vomiting rag doll is ripping off his gas mask in a state of semi-consciousness. I look over my shoulder to see the medics sticking the oxy viva on him as we stagger on. To all of our amazement, he recovers, and not only does he recover, but with his team, they actually catch up and pass a couple of the other teams. We are now directed to cross a mud and clay pit, the remanence of a demolished brick factory. The clay pit was the dumping pond for the waste during the brick manufacturing process.

One of the DS barks out: "Do not get the logs wet."

This means only one thing: balance the log on your shoulder or above your head if you are vertically challenged, whatever it takes but don't get that fucking log wet crossing the clay pit. It will suck up the water and weigh even more.

As we cross the quagmire, guys disappear below the slush with just their arms sticking up holding the log up out of the water, only to reappear spluttering for air as they step up out of the unseen hole underfoot. I am just too fucking knackered to laugh at what is really a comical sight. The mud stinks from years of effluent and other crap that had been dumped in it. I'm just shy of 5' 10," not tall. My turn, and I disappear into the quagmire only to re-emerge spitting out mud and trying to catch my breath, my legs burning from the lactic acid build up as I try to push through the sucking mud. But at least the tear gas has stopped burning or is it that everything else is hurting more?

Reaching the other side, we now have to climb up out of the mud pit, keeping the log off the ground of course. In typical style, the DS has chosen the steepest incline for us to climb up. Too bad if you're the bloke on the back end of the log as you get all the weight transfer as the angle increases on the climb up the side of the bank. You guessed, out goes the call yet again.

"Gas, gas, gas."

We cross the mud pit at least three times. The rest is a blur. I think I may have carried the brick at some stage on one of the laps around the clay pit – can't be sure. My brain has switched off, numbed from the physical and mental flogging endured in the past week. Jogging, well more like a shuffle, on the spot still holding the log, both my shoulders rubbed red raw from the log bouncing up and down off them and my arms are screaming, trembling from the weight of the log and fatigue. Where I had ripped off the callouses from the rope burn, I have developed new ones and my hands are now numb as well. Standing in front of the gates to the

Maylands Police Academy, this has to be the end – *there's not much more they can do to us, surely?* Everyone is fucked; we are so exhausted and the exercises impossible to complete and actually served no purpose other than to fuck with our spirits. But that was the objective. Then the senior DS walks up, looks all of us up and down with a sneer on his face and informs us that he has just witnessed one of the most pitiful efforts he has ever seen on a TRG selection course. The TRG motto is 'Team-Work' and we have displayed none. And with that we are told:

"You're going back around again."

I want to explode and yell out 'FUCK' with the frustration and exhaustion I am feeling right now. Immediately, two of the starring candidates spit the dummy and drop their log. The rest of us resign ourselves to the fact we are going around again, doubting that was even physically possible, but nonetheless, we are hobbling ourselves around into position about to head off back down the road when I hear the most wonderful words one could hear.

"End ex, end ex."

End of Exercise. It is over; we have finished. Selection is over. The two lads who just spat the dummy have failed. So close to finishing and who knows maybe even passing and getting a jersey. It is all part of the mind games designed to see who has and who does not have the mental and intestinal fortitude to go that bit further, push on, and not give up. I have pushed myself further than I have ever thought possible and then some and then found a bit more when I was asked. The sense of achievement and pride that goes with passing selection is something you never forget and the physical and mental torture something you hope you never have to call upon again.

That's me on the last day of the TRG selection course. Only a couple of other candidates were to get a jersey this day. DS#1 in black far right back row.

    The 'Trigg Riot' is a night I had to call upon that same mental and physical toughness that I had found from deep within myself on the selection course.

    Crouching down behind a Police vehicle with my team, I look around at the scene of carnage. It is raining bricks, bottles, whatever our fine upstanding youth of the community can find to hurl at their protectors, the Police. A beer keg is launched through a windscreen of a Police van parked up in the street that brings cheers and laughter from the crowd. Cops going toe to toe with drunken shit heads, the battle is in full swing. I get on my two-way and call VKI for urgent backup: "Oscar five, require urgent backup. FUCKING NOW!" I scream at the two-way radio to emphasise the urgency.

    I pop my head up over the bonnet of the police car for a quick look and duck back down as another missile flies overhead, smashing another windscreen. The kids cheer and punch the air with their fists. Their parents would be so proud. We are outnumbered and effectively impotent to do anything without the right equipment and numbers.

Then, suddenly, blackness sweeps across me. Lights out. I didn't see it coming. Something thrown from somewhere within the melee, someone got lucky and found their mark. Me. Knocked out cold, unconscious. Coming out of the darkness and hitting me fair and square in the head is one of the tap spears, pulled from the beer kegs, as I was later informed. As my head recoils, my legs try desperately to keep me standing upright but buckle from underneath and then, darkness again and I'm out cold. Then, someone is holding me up. I can feel hands under my arm pits as I am dragged away face down. My head is a dead weight. I've got no strength in my neck to lift it up. I must look like one of those toys that sit on the dash of a car with the oversize wobbly head bobbling around. I certainly feel like one. I know I am trying to make myself walk but the legs are having none of it. Operator #29, my team partner, showing complete disregard for his own safety, has picked me up and is dragging me to safety as missiles rain down. In a very courageous and ballsy move, he put his own welfare at risk, and I am forever grateful to him. He and I held the record at the time in TRG for the number of crunches and chin-ups done in two minutes. He pipped me on the crunches if I remember rightly. Now a Sergeant and having also served his country in the UN, I pay my respects to this man.

I must have passed out again as I am bought back to consciousness with a searing pain between my shoulder blades. I cry out. "Get me off, get me off."

I am propped up against the wheel of one of the police patrol vehicles. The wheel hub is red hot from being driven at warp speed, as you do when your brothers in blue are in trouble. With some help as my legs are still not cooperating, I clamber up onto the back seat of the police car and pass out again. I don't know how long I am out, but I come to with someone touching my face and eyes. *I can't see, I can't see, I'm fucking blind.* I start to flap, pushing the hands way. *Who is it?*

"Get the fuck away from me?"

I prop myself up and open my eyes; a very cute young lady is wiping the blood out of my eyes that has run down from my head wound. *I never did get her phone number. Come on, I'm not one to ever miss an opportunity!* She looks a little bewildered at me. I must look a sight, covered in blood, and when I tried to sit up, she says something about being a nurse and that I should really be going to hospital. All I know is I am having none of that bullshit. Bloody hell my head is throbbing, my forehead has its own pulse. I can feel the skin taut across my swollen brow. I must look like a Neanderthal. And my head feels disconnected from the rest of my body. Some of my team mates will say that is normal for me, the pricks.

Sitting up, I start to get my shit together. I can see much better now but am still a bit disorientated. I look down the street to see anarchy is ruling. I look out the back to see the cavalry has arrived and is forming up. Cops have come from all over the city and even further. Country cops have driven into suburban regions to look after *their* patch so the local city cops can attend the riot. Now it is time to take back control of the streets, and I wasn't about to miss out on that.

I wobble to my feet, grab a helmet and shield, subconsciously feeling my riot baton is still in its retainer on my left hip and my pistol is on the right. I form up with my team dressed in full regalia (riot gear). We march on the rioting crowd. When mob mentality takes over, psychologically, it is usual that they are incited by a few and it was these cretins, the Leaders, that we are after.

The TRG is about to make entry on the house to be demolished where the brave characters who were sitting on the roof chanting "kill the pigs" are now cowering inside. Where common sense kicked back in for those not too drunk or stupid to realise, they quickly make their departure, scampering off down the streets as they see us approaching. The heroes who fancy their chances are dealt with expediently and, for some, the light comes on and they too slither away into the night, no longer feeling so brave. We form up on the front door of the house. Team Leader, Operator #17, announces the presence of the TRG at the front door to those inside and requests entry. Of course, none is forthcoming. Well-rehearsed and practiced 'Method of Entry', or MOE, is executed on the front door and lounge room windows and within seconds the TRG has breached entry into another house. MOE is the methodology of mechanically breaching doors and windows to gain access using door rams and hooligan tools (a fancy crowbar) and window reamers (an iron bar used to smash glass out of a window frame). Cowering on the floor, even hiding in a wardrobe, I ID a couple of the shitheads that had been up on the roof.

As we go from room to room, the TRG has started the house demolition a little ahead of the planned date. Passed from team member to team member, these now not-so-brave, fine, upstanding members of our society are unceremoniously dumped outside to an awaiting conga line of police vans for their ride to the central lockup. As one miscreant is dragged out after another, I hear the whimpers of, "It wasn't me, sir," or "I didn't do it."

One even said, "I was trying to stop them," among other pitiful excuses.

"I'm sorry, sir," are more of the whines that come from these pricks and yet only a few hours ago they are willing a drunken mob of several hundred to "Kill the pigs."

For the next couple of hours, I join the riot teams sweeping up and down the streets, clearing them of drunken shitheads and filling up the waiting police vans. We move in an extended line down the street, giving the order to disperse: "Police move, Police move."

We strike out with our batons from behind our riot shields, stepping over debris on the road – broken bottles, bricks and mashed letter boxes – pushing the rioters back down the street. As we walk, this young fella challenges me. I can't believe it. Here I am, dressed in Police uniform, stained with my own blood, carrying a riot shield, wearing a riot helmet and swinging a baton yelling, "Police, move!" and he shapes up to me with his fists. I am in no mood for this dickhead, and I am very pissed off.

"Mate, put your fists down and fuck off now, I am warning you."

But no. He wants to stand me up and try his luck. The *Lite Strike* spun-aluminium riot baton is a great pacifier. Weighing around 400 grams and 26 inches long, it delivers a blow that will cause localised pain, resulting in incapacitation. In other words, it fucking hurts if you get hit with it. I give him one more chance to go, but no, he stood his ground. *Reckon I could be dealing with this dickhead again in the future!*

I strike out with my baton aiming the tip of the baton at one of his fists. I re-adjust his attitude and he quickly retreats into the night. I name my baton 'Milo'. *It's marvellous what a difference Milo makes. Okay, who's next? Does anyone else want a taste of Milo?*

By the end of the night, there are several police cars and vans wrecked – panels kicked in, windows shattered, blue lights ripped off the roofs, even headlights and taillights kicked in. The roads and gardens are littered with broken bottles and bricks. Later in news reports, the media likened it to a scene from Beirut. After about three hours, I finally decide it is time to go to hospital. I have a splitting headache.

My Police issue Baton 'Milo' after the Trigg Riot. A few dings and dents but still making a difference.

Runover

From time to time, if we aren't doing counter terrorism training or kicking in doors of bank robbers, drug dealers or some nut job threatening to kill everyone, we would have to justify our existence by doing general policing duties. So, on this particular evening, I am driving and my partner, Operator #21, a former SASR soldier, are patrolling through the Perth CBD when he scopes a stolen vehicle in the traffic. Here we are, looking across at six of our indigenous brethren sitting in a car they should not be driving. We all take a double look at each other. Quite humorous really. It was like looking at a car full of the Black & White Minstrels. Wide eyes stare at one another and the chase is on, but it comes to an abrupt end in the heavy evening traffic, stopped by a set of red traffic lights on St George's Terrace, the main street of the Perth CBD. The doors spring open and a starburst of kaka's run from the stolen Commodore. I choose the driver and Operator #21 goes for one of the passengers. I run across the road and slip on the oil in the middle of the lane and go tits up, just as the lights turn green and the traffic starts to move off from the intersection. As I pick myself up off the road to continue the foot chase, I am T-boned by a car. Our little blue light on the roof of our unmarked patrol car and pitiful siren, lost in the sea of headlights and noise of city rush hour traffic, is of no use in alerting the workers and shoppers of our presence. No doubt the driver's attention was on the traffic and not anticipating seeing a cop fallen over in the middle of the road. Pissed off at myself for falling over, as I get to my feet in a half crouching position, in my peripheral something catches my eye and instinctively I thrust my arm out to fend off whatever it is. Maybe the driver from the stolen car has come back to stick the boot in when he saw me slip over? It is certainly not because I thought I could stop a car. As we collide, I see the expression on the driver's face like *'Oh shit! I've just run over a cop!'* His knuckles white as he clutches the steering wheel and his jaw drops, eyes like saucepans.

My Beretta 9mm pistol takes the brunt of the force to my hip from the front of the vehicle as my hand plants into the centre of the vehicle's bonnet. Then everything starts to spin like a kaleidoscope of colours. Red taillights, white headlights, amber indicators, multi-coloured neon lights of the city office buildings and streetlights as I tumble down the road. Instinctively, I tuck my arms and head in as I feel myself rolling over and over and over, hitting the kerbing in the centre median strip and finally coming to a rest in the middle of St George's Terrace. The kaleidoscope of colours still spins around in my eyes. Strangely, I can feel no pain. *Maybe I am numbed already from the broken bones?*

My partner, Operator #21, has witnessed it all. In his later recount of the incident, he reckons I cannoned off the car and was knocked down the road about twenty metres. I land on the median strip sitting upright, and look around like a stunned mullet. From where I have come to rest, I look across the road and, waiting at a bus stop, office workers stand dumbfounded, looking at me. I am alive, let alone uninjured. *Hey, I'm thinking the same. Don't' worry, I'm a lucky bastard.* The driver of the car who has hit me runs over and starts to apologise profusely. My mind is still back up the road somewhere tumbling over and over and had not caught up with the rest of my body yet, so I am not taking in too much of what is being said. I hear muffled talking, that's about it. I stand up and re-adjust my uniform. Not a scratch on me. The chequered wood pistol grip of my Beretta has got a big scrape across it and the leather holster is looking a little worse for wear with bits of bitumen embedded into the basket-weave leather work. Operator #21 tells me that the bonnet of the car I have ineptly tried to fend off is buckled in, evidently from where I had planted my hand. *Hmm, maybe not such a bad effort after all. Hope he's insured!* I quickly brush of the voiced concerns for my welfare from the gathering late-night shoppers, reassuring them, "I'm okay, I'm okay, thank you."

Sheepishly, I get back into our patrol vehicle, embarrassed for slipping over on the road and we head for the office. Notch one up to the crooks this night.

'Fragged'

At the TRG you train hard and play hard and we train for keeps. There's an old but true saying 'Train as ye shall play' and this certainly applies with the TRG. I suffered more injuries at training than I ever did on the job.

On this particular day, we are training at our live fire range complex which consists of a 'Kill House' and aircraft 'Mock-Up'. This is where we practice our MOE, team and individual tactics and clearance drills for both high risk domestic incidents and CT (Counter Terrorism) response. The training facility was gifted to the TRG from the SASR when they replaced their old 'Kill House' with a multimillion-dollar range complex down at Swanbourne as the Regiment went into their 'Black Role' (CT) full tilt. PC (political correctness) had found its way into both the Regiment and the TRG as the 'Kill House' was now to be known as the '360 range'. It had already found its way into mainstream policing.

As a weapons instructor at the Police Academy, I was to witness the incredulous decision, made by politicians no less, that Police apparently did not need to be trained to shoot at targets that looked anything like a human. *WTF!* A compromise was reached and so it came to pass that Police from now on would be trained to shoot at a grey shape that took the appearance like that of a coffin. *Oh, the irony.*

The TRG 'Kill House' is a structure of sheets of inches thick steel as the skin of the walls with three layers of 'Stramit,' a compressed straw boarding, lining the inside. The 'Stramit' absorbs projectiles preventing ricochet and the steel skin prevents the rounds exiting the structure. Over time, as the 'Stramit' breaks down, individual sheets can be pulled out and replaced. Inside, the rooms can be configured with partitioning to whatever shape, with inward and outward opening doors, no doors, lighting, darkness, furnished or unfurnished with multiple hostage and terrorist targets to simulate *shoot-don't-shoot* scenarios and, of course, accuracy of shot. The 'Kill House' can take 9mm and 40cal rounds, as well as distraction and tear gas grenades. An exhaust/extraction system in the roof vents off the smoke and cordite. After a day of training the smell still hangs heavily in the air (I grow to love the smell of cordite stinging my nostrils) with the empty bodies of distraction grenades and thousands of rounds of expended 9mm and 40cal brass casings littering the floor.

The 'aircraft mock-up' stood adjacent to the Kill House and was built of the same materials and simulated the interior of a passenger airline, bus or a train. It's a great training facility and we were very lucky to have it and are still fortunate to be able to get down to Swanbourne and use their awesome facilities from time to time. Gradually, our training ramps up from clean fatigues and dry fire drills to full CT Battle Dress and, Live Fire CQB (Close Quarter Battle) tactics.

Training culminates in a couple of exercises that are designed to test everyone's and the group's capabilities. It is the final exercise. We are to breach the door on the Kill House and clear multiple rooms, engaging identified terrorist targets and save the lives of the hostages. In our stack (tactical formation entry team), we are given the green light (order to commence operations) and distractions are thrown on entry. Distractions or Sound and Flash (SF) grenades are a less lethal grenade that emits a high decibel sound and white phosphorous flashes designed to stun and disorientate anybody in a room. It scrambles the senses of the terrorists for a few vital seconds to allow the team to regain the tactical advantage upon entry. They are even more effective when deployed in the middle of the night.

The body of the grenade has port holes where the sound and flash are emitted on igniting. The TRG generally used SF3's or SF6's, and we also had some old SF9's meaning this model had nine portholes (nine flashes and nine bangs) and this older model discharged plastic caps that contained the pyrotechnics from within the body of the grenade. We use the old SF9's to simulate an IED (Improvised Explosive Device) in training. The bleeding hearts reckon the SF9 is too 'aggressive' to use on real jobs. *Fuck me, tell that to a terrorist or drug crazed lunatic trying to stab you. Don't the armchair critics realise that these things can actually save lives by using them?*

We clear the first room and set up on the second door to the next room. Covering the door to the next room, I wait only a few seconds as another operator nods to me and cracks the door.

"Police, Police, get down, get down," I yell through my gas mask on making entry into the room.

Sweeping my SMG (Sub Machine Gun) across the room from right to left as I turn heavy left – meaning the room structure was such that it was all to the left of the door where I immediately come upon a wardrobe, prop and cover as the rest of the team makes entry behind me, covering their areas of responsibility and clearing the room of terrorists. Anything where a person can hide is basically treated like another room. This wardrobe has two doors so requires another operator to open it. Listening to the controlled fire at identified terrorist targets, I know someone will be on my shoulder any second once they had accounted for all the terrorists. Then *bang, bang, bang, bang, bang, bang, bang, bang, bang*... someone has thrown another distraction grenade ... or so I thought. *That's louder than usual*, I think. *Someone has thrown a 9 instead of a 6, oops, not to worry.*

Still covering the wardrobe with my SMG, I smell smoke and then the pain hits me. A SF9 distraction has been set up as a booby trap to simulate an IED – a trip wire running across the doorway, and the distraction on the floor in front of the wardrobe. I was standing astride of it. Somehow, I have missed the trip wire and, as the rest of the team has made entry behind me, one of the guys has tripped the wire, releasing the spoon and pin that ignites the distraction. I look down to see my fatigues, chard, blackened and smouldering. The SF9 has gone off right next to my left leg. I can see a mush of pink flesh in the blackened chard material of my smouldering fatigues. *Lucky the pods don't shoot upwards.*

I call out from under my gas mask, "No duff, no duff, no duff."

'No Duff' is called out loud three times. It is the verbal call in the event of an out of exercise incident or real injury.

I hobble over to a wall and slide down to a seated position, back against the wall, out of the way of the boys. The team is still clearing the rest of the Kill House and I want to stay out of their way on the fight back as they will return clearing all the rooms again before taking up positions of dominance around the house. On my call of No Duff, the DS enters the room and takes one look at my leg.

"End Ex, End Ex."

This brings the exercise effectively to an end.

I call out, "Medic, Medic."

I take a closer look at my leg. The distraction has cauterised the flesh just below the calf muscle and does it fucking hurt! There is a hole about the size of a fifty-cent piece and about 3cm deep. Funny, I have smelt dead, rotting bodies before, and it's a smell you can't get out of your nostrils, let alone your uniform. But I had not smelt burnt flesh before. It's a mix of that metallic blood taste, pungent singed hair and raw mincemeat. I poke the pulp and the melted material of my fatigues that had cauterised together. Then I remember, *that's right, I am the designated team medic for today ... Bugger.*

Well, you can imagine the look on the face of the triage nurse at the hospital.

"What happened to you?" she enquires looking at me quizzically.

"Umm ... a grenade blew a hole in my leg," I reply.

"A what?"

I go on to explain and she realises that I'm not some dickhead making up a story to get drugs. She asks me if it's hurting.

"A bit, I guess." I smile back at her.

"On a scale of one to ten?" she asks, standing up and peering over the glass partition to look at my leg.

I tell her about an eight. She just shakes her head as I sit at the triage counter talking to her through the glass partition. But nothing is more painful than what is to come next: debridement of the wound.

It's about an hour or so later, after triage, that I am called down to the casualty ward for treatment. I am sitting on a bed in a cubicle of the casualty ward with my leg up when the locum steps in and places a sterile tray of assorted goodies next to the bed. Gloved up, he opens a few different packets, first cutting away the remains of the lower portion of my fatigues and dropping them into a brown medical wastes bag hanging on the side of the trolley next to him. Then he wipes around the wound with betadine antiseptic leaving that yellow brown stain.

"Is that tender?" he asks.

"Not too bad," I reply as I take an interest in one particular item on the tray.

"Okay, I'm going to use a little local anaesthetic in the wound before we debride."

What? Wait! Now, he's got my full attention. In the TRG we have the opportunity to do a trauma medic course, learning how to suture, put an IV (Intravenous needle) in and give injections. Really cool stuff, so naturally I was interested, but debride was a term I have not heard.

He goes on, "You're going to need a skin graft to fix this up but first we have to debride the wound."

"What's debride?" I quiz, pointing at the scrubbing sponge.

He explains that basically he's going to scrub the wound with a wire brush to remove the dirt and dead flesh. A debrider looks like a sponge with steel wool on one side, like what you use to wash the pots and pans at home – well the ladies do anyway. This is what is in the packet that had caught my eye earlier. After a few winces with the needle going into the wound to anaesthetise the flesh, the doctor starts on the debriding. Not the soft sponge side, that's for him to hold, but with the steel wool side.

Ow, that hurt. I whimper and my leg twitches. Casually, the doctor says, "Oh, sorry … is that a little sensitive?"

Nodding my head, I purse my lips and my eyes start to water. And so we went, for about fifteen minutes, with him debriding, me twitching when he touched a raw spot and him giving a bit more local to numb the area. Let me tell you, hospitals are not my favourite place because you're there for two reasons, one you are crook or someone you know is and I am not keen on either option, least of all when the doctor starts talking about admitting me to a ward overnight.

I manage to convince the doctor that I am okay and I need to go back to training tomorrow and finish the course. I promise I will come back at the end of the course to have the wound grafted. With a sideways glance, he plugs the hole up with this gel like stuff, sticks some plastic skin film over the top and gives me some Panadol Forte for the pain and jabs me full of antibiotics and a tetanus shot for good measure. *Sadistic prick.*

The next day, sporting new training fatigues, I return to training with a shin guard covering my wound and popping Panadol every few hours as the pain returns throughout the day. That bit I don't tell the DS. The following Monday I go into hospital for a skin graft to the wound. Even now I can push my thumb into the hole in my leg down to the first joint.

Most people who have received a blow to the head like I had in the 'Trigg Riot' would have been dead, or at least had a fractured skull, so I was told by the medicos who treated me at QEII hospital later on in the early morning of the night before. I still bare the scar on my head today.

The resulting dent in the bonnet of the car caused by my 'fend off', broken bones would normally result and getting a hole blown in your leg would see you on crutches, but no, not this little black duck. I am not trying to make myself out to be some macho man or big tough guy – what I am saying is that I am driven, motivated, determined and stubborn, which sees me get through these sorts of things. What I lack in mental or physical aptitude and skill, I make up with pure determination and dependability.

My escapades had come to earn me the nickname of 'Block', sometimes 'Blockhead', or 'Blocker'. Block seemed to be the preferred of everyone, and so it was to pass that I came to be known as 'Block'. Personally, I think it has more to do with my big mug head. Well, there you have it. Now you know a bit more about 'Block'.

Now to recant some more memorable stories of my personal experiences.

CT/CQB Team dressed in Tactical Assault Order. That's me. HK MP5 9mm SMG in hand

That's me – Operator #30

Clandestine Drug Operation - HK G43 5.56/223 Field Rifle

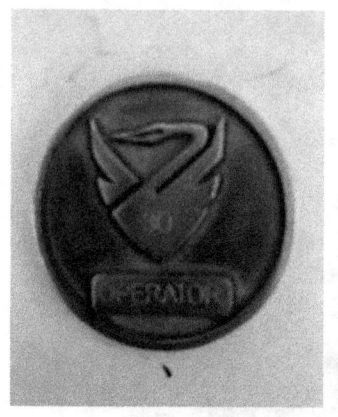 

TRG Operator Coin #30

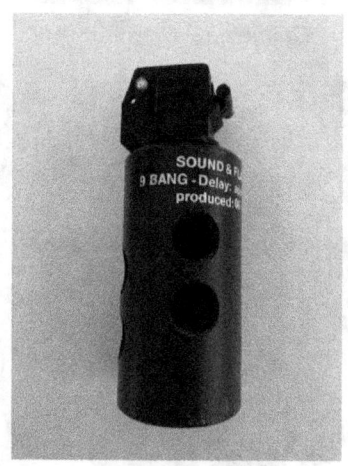

'Fragged' SF 9

Chapter 2

Hostage Rescue

A beautiful Autumn Sunday: you know, that fresh, crisp, clean air, bright sun but not hot, bluest of blue skies and not a cloud in sight. I am the On-Call TC (Tactical Commander) for the week. It is my job to attend and assess any incident after hours and, if warranted, activate the on-call team, the extra pay for being on call being well spent on renovating the family home.

Today, I am enjoying my time with my absolutely gorgeous two-year-old daughter playing with her *Play-do*, making spaghetti hair for her dolls when my pager goes off – some cunt has just bought an end to my glorious weekend. Jumping into the 'War Wagon', I notify VKI that I am en-route, Category B, meaning lights & sirens but stopping at red TCL's (Traffic Control Lights) and stop signs.

"Oscar 3 on this channel."

"Roger, Oscar 3. We have a mother holding her son hostage. Locals are in attendance. ETA?"

I reply, "About 20 out. Can you call PET, Negs and SJA out please?"

PET being the Psychiatric Emergency Team, Negs are the Police negotiators and SJA are St John's Ambulance Service.

Why does it have to be today, on a weekend of all days? But I know that there are more domestic incidents on weekends, especially on Sundays when families get together and the looneys go right off – especially if it's a full moon – I kid you not. Nurses and ambos will tell you the same. Something to do with the moon, tides, gravity and the poles upset the equilibrium of those so inclined, so it goes. Hence where the term, 'Lunatic' (lunar) derives from.

Cutting the siren as I get closer, I pull into the street. There is the local Police van parked across the road blocking traffic and another one at the other end of the street. No media as yet – it would appear they must be enjoying this glorious Sunday as much as I was. There's about a half dozen neighbours in the street in deep discussion, all looking at the *Stronghold*. The *Stronghold'* is the code word we give to identify the building where the incident is taking place.

The local Sergeant comes up and gives me a Sit-Rep (Situation Report/update): Mum is a paranoid schizophrenic and has been off her meds for about a week. Her son is five years old. They are in the bathroom and he has two of his boys talking to her, keeping her calm. She has a pair of dressmaker's scissors and is threatening to stab her son. Making my mental notes, we are abruptly interrupted by the son's father, understandably very distraught and frantic.

"Do anything, *anything* to get my son out, please," he begs me. "I give you permission to kill her. I just want my son back."

Whoa! Okay, he's obviously upset. "Okay sir, please go with the Sergeant."

I steer him to the Sergeant who ushers him away. I walk back to the war wagon and get on the radio to VKI and activate the on-call team.

Still in my civvies (shorts and t-shirt), quietly I enter the typical Aussie 70s-style house and can just make out voices coming from the rear. I make my way through to the laundry and, through the open doorway, I can just make out the two GD (General Duties) lads sitting on chairs a few feet back from the bathroom, talking to the mother. I can see that the laundry opens up onto an enclosed patio area backing onto the garden and the bathroom runs off the patio to the right. The GD guys are doing an awesome job keeping her calm and reassuring the son. I can see she is holding the scissors to her boy's neck. Poor little bugger doesn't know any better and is happy sitting on mum's lap. She is sitting on the toilet next to the vanity. There's an array of knives lined up for her selection on top of the vanity. I could see that the two GD boys have their revolvers. *Okay, good.* In this day and age, there were still cops around who didn't or wouldn't carry a gun. I back out of the laundry and work my way around through the house to look at alternative entry and exit points to the bathroom. As I go, I draw a mental map of the floor plan of the house and start to put an EA (Emergency Action) plan together with various tactical options. Satisfied that I had enough to go on with, and time being critical, I head back outside to the war wagon, get changed into my fatigues and start pulling out the on-call team bags. I drag the 'war chest' out for the force options – gas, bean bag rounds, shields and SMG's. I get my kit on and go over to the Sergeant. He is in charge.

I run the plan past him and, if he approves, I will take control of the tactical operation. He remains in charge overall as the senior officer on-scene. He is cool with the plan. The on-call team arrives and as they kit up, I fill them in on the situation: two operators to the rear of the house to cover the door from the patio enclosure, two to the entry from the patio/bathroom into the dining/kitchen area and three of us into the laundry. I keep in mind the risk of crossfire, but it's the best option given the circumstances and I know the boys are well trained and disciplined with their muzzle awareness and trigger discipline.

Everyone has eyes on the two GDs and the bathroom door, but we stay out of sight of mum and son. My idea is that we contain the situation, hold our positions until the 'Negs' can take over from the GD boys and, with the expertise of the PET, get a peaceful resolution. Our role is to remain on standby in case a force option is needed as a last resort.

Something I am to learn afterwards is that mentally disturbed persons senses become acute while others dull. Hearing becomes acute, sense of smell dulls. The mother is now talking in tongues. It's scary weird religious cult stuff, talking a million miles an hour in some strange alien-like language, speaking to her god and giving him a right ear bashing by the sounds of it. Whatever it was, I don't know; maybe we made some noise as we established our positions, maybe she just snapped, I don't know, but I hear one of the GD guys yelling out, "Oh god no, don't do that!"

As I look out of the laundry door to the right, I see a blur of blue clutching the boy as they scramble away towards the lounge area of the house. It has gone to shit. *Fuck!* No time for a squeeze down and the usual protocols.

I just yell, "Go! Go! Go!"

The boys didn't need telling as they were already on the move and we head for the bathroom, not even time to grab a shield. Just our personal kit. Time had run out for us and the boy.

Standing there in the middle of the bathroom with the biggest pair of fuck-off dressmaker's scissors I have ever seen, mum is repeatedly stabbing herself in the chest and stomach in frenzied lunges, all the while talking in tongues to whatever higher being she is in contact with. Blood is pissing out everywhere.

First at the door, I've drawn my pistol when the commotion started; not that I would shoot her now anyway. Operator #23 reaches over the top of my right shoulder extending his arm forward with a can of OC (Oleoresin Capsicum, better known as Pepper Spray) spray and lets her have it. She is drenched in the stuff, looks like she'd taken a shower in orange citrus juice. We take a pregnant pause in the doorway. This is our chance. Our priority now is saving her life. Bugger me how things can change in an instant. Myself, Operator #23 and #35 jump on her and I make a reach for the scissors, knocking them out of her hand.

Nothing pretty about it. Legs and arms flailing, the force of three men wearing basic tac (tactical) order, knock her to the floor. Now I weigh about 105kg and so do #23 & #35, plus we're wearing probably another five or so kilos on our assault order (pistol, mags, OC spray, spare mags, radio, steel handcuffs, knife, baton, mobile phone) so she has around three hundred and fifty kilos on top of her.

A symptom of mental illness can be phenomenal strength. Mentally disturbed people can exhibit extreme strength because the brain and body are not working in a normal capacity. Mum just rises from the floor like a woman possessed and throws us off like rag dolls. It's scary stuff, like a scene from the Omen with her talking in some alien language. We leap back on, the mix of her blood and OC spray is making it very difficult to get a grip on her arms and a solid footing on the bathroom tiles, slipping and sliding around in the mix of blood and spray. We try to get her hands behind her back to get the flexi cuffs on, but she just locks her arms out. Her strength is unbelievable, even impressive, dare I say. The OC is starting to kick in, not on her, on us. I begin to cough, trying to suck in the air. My eyes are scratchy, and I can feel the skin around my neck burning. We all fall to the ground again struggling to keep hold of an arm, and #35 attempting to get the cuffs on. Still talking in tongues, she starts to smash her face into the floor all the while fighting with the strength of ten men. #23 gives her a knee into her side to knock the wind out of her and this seems to slow her down momentarily. With all three of us on top of her and desperately hanging onto her arms, we manage to get them behind her back and close enough together to pull on the flexi cuffs over her hands and bind them together. All three of us are coughing and spluttering from the effects of the OC and we're covered in this mad bitch's blood. My eyes balls feel like someone is rubbing them with sandpaper. #23 and #35 look like they are suffering as I am, their eyes blood shot, red and puffy, snot hanging out of their noses and looking like poms on holiday who had spent too long in the Australian sun. I don't say anything, I am too fucking knackered from fighting mum. I guess they are too. The ambo's come into the bathroom and promptly take a step back out as they get a whiff of the OC.

#17 makes the suggestion, "Hook her under the arms and we'll drag her out of here."

And with that we all lift her up. She's a big woman. We stand the mother up and stagger out of the bathroom, through the patio and outside into the back garden. We sit her down on a plastic chair and the ambos get to work on her wounds.

I cough and spit out lumps of mucous and blow snot out of my nose, blinking profusely to lubricate and soothe my eyes. I get a flash back to that last day on selection and understood why we had been put through such an experience. Three big men, all dressed in our tactical finery, bent over in the garden, crying like big girls. I look at #23 and #35: they look a right sight. The front of the mother's dress is shredded, and she has some serious-looking wounds to her chest. Then to my amazement, all of a sudden, it is like someone has flicked a switch.

Looking around at all the commotion and suffering the indignity of her being handcuffed, she glances around and queries, "What's that funny smell?"

This is the sum total of the effect that the OC has had upon her – zero– all she can recollect of the whole incident as it appears. I look at #23 and #35 and shake my heads in disbelief, and to shake the boogies off hanging from my nose.

I am to find out later that the mother had in fact stabbed her son with the dressmaker's scissors, thrusting the blades down into his neck and just nicking his heart. The two GD guys managed to snatch the boy from her as she raised the scissors for a second lunge into his young body, a display of absolute courage by the GDs and with complete disregard for their own safety. That was the commotion I'd heard from the laundry as I saw the guys grab the son and make a run for it. Thankfully, the son survived his wounds.

After hosing myself down in the backyard to wash off the worst of the blood and OC, we pack up our toys into the war wagon and head to the Cannington CIB (Criminal Investigations Branch) office for a handover and debrief. Standing around in the car park at the back of the office before the debrief, we discuss the merits of OC and its effects on the mentally disturbed. I guess it has served its purpose in as much that it did distract her to a point that allowed us to take her to the ground and disarm her. The local detective, now in charge of the ensuing investigation, and whom I know from when we were junior constables in Fremantle, comes out to talk to us.

"G'day, Fitzy."

"G'day, Block. Boys, bit of a problem. The father has lodged a complaint."

"What? You're fucking kidding! About what?" I am incredulous.

Fitzy goes on to tell us: "He's alleging you caused her facial injuries; assaulted her. She has some broken teeth and a broken nose."

I set the record straight and tell Fitzy about her old man telling me I had his permission to kill his wife, to rescue his son and how she smashed her own face on the bathroom floor during her psycho rage.

"Make sure you put that in your statements, boys. Come inside for a brew and we'll do this debrief."

We hear no more about the alleged assault on the mum. The two police officers' actions no doubt saved the life of the boy today and we probably saved the life of the mum. Yet the father is ignorant to all of this and has the audacity to make a complaint against us. *Un-fucking believable*. I arrive home and give my daughter the biggest hug and savour that smell only a parent knows of their own child. It is still a beautiful Sunday. How could anybody do harm to their own child? It is something I cannot fathom.

Post-incident, I was to learn that the father had found his faith in God, Mum is back on her medication and the family is living happily forever after. *Well, isn't that just dandy. All is forgiven, until next time!*

Chapter 3

Suicide by Cop

We are not always successful, and I am gutted that I, we, the TRG, failed to save the life of a man on this particular day. It may sound strange or contrary in the mind of the lay person that the TRG saves lives as opposed to killing terrorists. What must be remembered is we are Police first and foremost. But, make no mistake, I will take the life of another in order to save my own or that of someone else when necessary.

Called to a house on the outskirts of Perth, Operator #7 and I were met by two very distressed parents. Their son has not been seen or heard from all day. This is out of character for him according to the parents. No rhyme or reason to think anything untoward until the father discovers his Ruger model 10 .22 semi auto rifle is missing. #7 goes through all the usual questioning of the parents about their son and comes up with not much apart from the description and registration of the son's car. This is a worry. In my experience, those who threaten suicide or self-harm and leave notes or act out is a cry for help. All the suicides I have attended, the individual has just gone ahead and done it. I get onto VKI and put out a LOTBKF (Look Out To Be Kept For) for the son's car. Mates, relatives, his work are all contacted, but no one has seen sight nor sound of him. Not much we can do but hope he comes home and there is a simple explanation.

Later in the day, local Police come across the son parked up in his car on a bush track in the Perth foothills. He has the .22 calibre rifle and promptly tells the two uniform cops to "Fuck Off', which they oblige and call for backup. Because we have issued the initial LOTBKF, VKI advise us and we attend. The local boys are at the entrance to the bush track that runs off from a picnic area at the popular Gosnells Rock Pools. #7 tells the GD guys to establish this point as a Command Post and to get onto VKI and request call out of the TRG On-Call team, Ambo's, Negs and PET. More GDs arrive to place a cordon around the scene and control access by the public.

With that, #7 and I cautiously walk our way down the track until we get a glimpse of the vehicle. In Police blues, we stick out like dog's balls, so we go bush and carefully and slowly work our way through the dry scrub to get closer to where the son is parked up. The plan is to observe until our guys can get in behind him and consider a tactical option. I'm closest to the track and #7 is alongside to my right.

#7 whispers to me: "Block, can you see him, mate?"

I sneak a quick look. "Only just. Can't really make out what he's doing."

We edge a little closer, trying very hard not to be heard or seen. Conscious of this, we turn our radios down. Funny how every little sound seems to be magnified ten-fold when you don't want it to be.

"How about now, Block? Can you see him yet?" #7 enquires.

Again, I peek out from the bushes. But the sun reflecting off the windscreen obscures vision of the driver's seat.

"I think he's sitting in his car. Can't really tell for sure."

The bush track is for a single vehicle and one way only. He has chosen his location well. It's a warm bright day and the cicadas are going at it full time, chirping away. You can smell the bush, a mix of eucalyptus, wattle and dry heat. Surrounded by bush, it is going to be difficult and time consuming for our boys to get in close. We are going to have to try and buy time and offer some distraction to mask any noise they may make, allowing the boys to get in close and gas him out or overpower him somehow.

#7 and I agree that I should start communicating with him as I have some line of sight. A trained negotiator I am not, but I have done the Verbal Judo/Tactical Communications course. #7 will maintain comms with VKI, the on-call team and lead the tactical operation.

A dump of adrenalin and the heart rate goes up. *Deep breathe, okay, here I go.*

"Derek, it's the Police here, mate. Can you hear me?" I shout out from within the bushes.

We realise by doing this that we have compromised our location but there is no other option if we want to stall and buy some time. The other problem is that the bush really offers no cover from gunfire, only concealment. A lucky shot put our way and a .22 round can pass through a few bushes without too much trouble and we were well and truly in range.

No answer. I try again, "Derek, it's the Police. Can you talk to me?"

"Yeah, fuck off and leave me alone."

I have got an answer. *Okay, good, we have got a response from him.* Unsurprisingly, he is pissed off with the situation.

I ask the question: "Derek, what's the problem, mate? We want to help you?"

Comes back his curt reply: "Just fuck off and leave me alone, you pricks."

#7 whispers to me the boys are here and moving in behind, to keep talking and see if he has the rifle in his possession. I tell #7 I can't see and I'm going to have to move. #7 agrees.

Gradually, I inch across to my left, closer to the track, calling out to Derek to mask any noise I make moving through the bush. It's been a hot summer, and everything is tinder dry. Every leaf I brush past crackles, every branch is ready to snap. Underfoot the ground is hard, dry and dusty. Moving quietly is impossible.

I call out: "Derek, your mum and dad are worried, mate. They want you back home."

I can now make out most of the car, with the front of the vehicle facing us. The driver's side door is open, and I can just make out Derek sitting in the driver's seat.

"Derek, you're not in any trouble, mate. We're here because your mum and dad asked us to look for you," I try to reason with him.

"I said fuck off, you cunts, and let me do it," comes back Derek's reply.

"Leave you to do what, mate? What do you mean?"

I knew what he meant, but again I am trying to buy more time. Derek was pretty straight forward with his answer.

"You dumb cunts, I have the old man's rifle, now just fuck off and let me to get on with it."

Now we know for sure he does have the rifle; he is suicidal and we're not his favourite people right now.

#7 signals me to keep talking and whispers across to me, "Block, see if you can get him away from the car."

#7 is talking to the boys moving in through the bush and working on a plan to try and save Derek. Whatever that plan is I don't know but that's fine, I don't really need to. I just need to keep Derek distracted.

"Derek, I can't hear you to well, mate Can you get out of the car so we can talk, mate?"

As I ask Derek to do this, I edge a little bit further out so I can see if he gets out of the car and more importantly what he is doing with the rifle.

"Fuck off and you won't have to worry about talking to me" is his answer.

I've got myself right at the edge of the bush along the track. I can see the car and Derek now, but in doing so I have inadvertently showed myself to Derek, who instantly looks at me, with the rifle in his hand and he comes back at me.

"Fuck off I said, you cunts."

"Derek, we can get someone to come and talk to you, mate? Someone who can help you," I plead.

In a very definite and demanding statement Derek says, "Now fuck off."

He levels the rifle at me.

I look at #7 who is squatting down in the bushes about five or six feet away from me and I just launch myself in his direction – I didn't need to be told twice – getting scratched to shit diving through the dry bush and crash landing on my guts just short of #7.

"Fuck!" I say as I look up at #7, catching my breath. "He pointed the fucking rifle at me."

#7 is on the radio to the boys. I assume they are getting close and he is confirming that Derek has the rifle in his hand.

I scramble to a crouching position and yell out to Derek "Put the rifle down, mate. We can't talk if you have the rifle."

No answer.

"Derek, put the rifle back in the car."

There was no knowing now what Derek is doing or where he is. There's no response from him. Is he still near the car or is he heading our way … with the rifle? *Fuck, fuck, what to do.*

"Are the boys close?" I ask #7.

I'm going through the 'What ifs?'. What if he comes right at us? The Ruger 10 .22 is a very accurate rifle for a short-barrel weapon. With a ten-round box magazine, it will fire off all ten rounds as fast as you can pull the trigger. I know, I used to have one myself. I am well aware of the 'Suicide by Cop' syndrome whereby Police are forced into shooting an individual in self-defence.

#7 tells me the boys are almost there. Then, from the direction of the vehicle there is a short sharp crack. A gunshot. A .22 report.

Wide eyed and wide-mouthed, we look at each other in silence and wait. The cicadas have stopped and its eerily peaceful. *Was that fired in our direction?* There is no 'Thud, Thwack'.

When a projectile is fired from a rifle and finds its terminating point, there is the 'Thud' sound as the round hits its target, followed by the sound of the projectile fired from the rifle as it exits the muzzle, resulting in the 'Thwack'. If you count the time between the thud and the thwack, you can estimate how far away the shooter is. We wait. Nothing but silence. No 'Thud' means no terminating point of impact. Could only mean one thing. *Fuck*!

"Derek, you alright, mate? Derek?"

Nothing. *Shit.*

#7 tells the boys to hold their loc's.

"Block, we'll move down and have a look, mate." We have both drawn the same conclusion.

Derek has topped himself (no pun intended). With that, we gradually stand and draw our Berettas as we step out onto the track. Keeping low, I move across to the far side of the track to my left and #7 stays on the right next to the bush where we have been hiding. Moving forward, we reach Derek. He has shot himself through the head and dropped where he stood. The round has gone straight through and exited out the other side near his temple. There is a steady stream of blood, like a fountain, squirting out of the exit wound to his head.

#7 gets on the radio and calls for the ambos to be escorted down to our loc. We can't pronounce death, but you don't have to be a doctor to see Derek has achieved what he had intended. The fountain of blood has now slowed to a trickle pooling around his head and the rifle is lying in the dirt where he has fallen. I'm feeling frustrated, annoyed, even angry, a mix of emotions. Why do people do this? Surely things cannot be that bad that you have to take your own life. What a selfish thing to do, causing so much grief and distress to your family and friends. Don't they think about that. Bastard scared the fuck out of me when he pointed the rifle at me.

My train of thought is interrupted by our guys who had been crawling their way through the bush to surround Derek; they step out of the bushes at the rear of the car. As it turns out, the guys were almost there; only a few more minutes and it may have been a different ending. One option they had was to hit him with a mix of distraction grenades and *'Ferret'* tear gas rounds to knock him over and rush him should the opportunity arise, and he was not a threat to anyone, other than himself. (This incident occurred in the days preceding the TASER). The area was now a crime scene and subject to a coronial investigation. Still running through my head, I was trying to think of what else we could have done to stop this guy from committing suicide. I concluded that there was probably nothing we could do.

I was later quizzed by the uninformed. "Why didn't you shoot him when he pointed the rifle at you?"

In the totality of the circumstances, I truly believe that it was not Derek's intention to harm me. He either wanted Police to shoot and kill him or to scare me so we would 'Fuck Off', as he suggested we do. That had certainly worked, he scared the shit out of me, and he took the opportunity to kill himself.

Ruger Model 10/22 Semi Auto 10 round box magazine .22 calibre round

Chapter 4

Mongrel Dog

The WA Police Mounted Section (horses) has been around for a long time, used for ceremonial purposes, patrolling, searching and PR, but they come into their own for crowd control. A single horse is worth at least ten men.

K9 (Canine) was relatively new for WAPOL and again, dogs are great for sniffing out drugs and running down the crooks. We had trained with both the horses and dogs in crowd control/public order and now we were starting to use them in sieges. Brilliant! Send in a dog snarling and gnashing teeth, and, whilst it is unfortunate if the dog gets killed, the life of an officer has been potentially saved. Don't get me wrong, I love dogs I have grown up with dogs and have one in my own family I love them. But a Police Dog or K9 is a working animal. I know their handlers/trainers can become quite attached to the dog, which takes on the persona of a surrogate partner. But no one was going to get close to what can only be described as the 'Mongrel Dog'.

I am the Tactical Commander and the TRG has been called to a house where a drugged-up, boozed-up dickhead is threatening suicide and the usual "I'll kill the cops if they come near me" bullshit that accompanies such events. Negotiators are standing by for us to deliver the 'Power Ball'.

Not sure who came up with it but it's an ingenious idea. Over the years, we had delivered mobile phones in all manner of ways, sometimes successfully, other times not. Often the offender will rip the phone plug out of the wall in a fit of anger or just not answer his phone, and comms is important when negotiating. The Power Ball is a round cage made of heavy gauge wire. In the body of the Power Ball is a transceiver so the offender and Police can speak with one another. In addition, it is a siren for distraction to provide ourselves with a tactical advantage. The Power Ball is attached to a long power cable that's on a spindle and connected to a power source. It's built tough and has a bit of weight behind it and will easily shatter a lounge room window when hurled at one. With the power ball delivered, the Negs are talking to the man in the house and, whilst their primary goal is to seek a peaceful resolution, they can also gather useful intel for us.

Our boy alleges to have a syringe filled with poison or something that he will use to inject himself with and this has been confirmed by his family that he has a syringe with what they believe also to be filled with some sort of poison. My team is holding down the street at the FUP (Form Up Point) while we wait for Western Power to cut the electricity to the streetlights to provide us with the cover of darkness. The ambos have just arrived, as have K9. It is confirmed that there is no one else in the house and all are safe and accounted for. I head on over to the negotiators to listen in as to how the negotiations are going and get an opinion from the negotiator on the current state of mind of our boy. The Negs are awesome at what they do, more often than not, talking the offender into giving up peacefully. It can be a bit of an anti-climax for us when some wanker has beaten up their partner, trashed the house and threatening to kill us all and the weak prick gives up while we've been standing around for hours getting hungry and tired. Which is exactly what you really want to happen, of course.

Not that it always pans out that way – like the time negotiations broke down with a young fella and we were given a green light. The Neg had managed to talk the young guy outside to have a smoke and that's where we hit him. I come charging down the side of the house with a riot shield and helmet on with Operators #11 and #12 hanging on to my belt and pushing me as we went for extra hitting power. We've hit this guy with everything, knocking him clean off his feet and landing flat on top of him with his face pushed into the shield and the weight of all three of us on top of him. I just lay there looking at this guy, with his face squashed up against the polycarbonate riot shield, while the boys cuffed him. When I get up, the Neg is still standing there, casually enjoying his smoke and having a little chuckle to himself how we've flattened this guy to the ground.

This time though, I am talking to 'Col', the negotiator, who used to be a TRG member and we were partnered up for a while before he decided to leave to be a detective and now a negotiator. Great guy. He has a good understanding of our tactics and therefore what information we need from the tactical aspect. Col tells me that our man is still threatening self-harm and, with that, I head back to my team, give them a sitrep and an EA plan. An EA is an Emergency Action – what we are going to do if it goes to shit quickly.

As the situation progresses, we put in place a DA (Deliberate Action) Plan. This is what we do, at our call and choosing. I then head over to the K9 and intro myself to the handler and let him know what the current status is. His dog is sitting quietly next to him. The K9 are on a different radio net to the one we operate on, DVP (Digital Voice Protected) which means all anyone else hears is 'White Noise'. I can talk on the net to my team but not K9, which means for the next hour or so I am going back and forth between my team, K9 and Col, which is fine, no great hassle. Back to Col for an update and he's no further ahead. Back to update my team.

"The DA Plan is that the K9 will make entry first. #27, you're door man, I want bean bag and OC on point, that'll be you two,

#31 and #9. Questions?"

None were forthcoming and off I went back to see how Col was progressing with talking to the man.

"Block, not getting anywhere with this guy at the moment. Let's see how we go for the next ten minutes or so you will you."

No problem, if the TRG do not have to commit to making entry then all the better for everyone all round. Every time I speak to the K9 handler I make sure to approach slowly and in a friendly manner and staying on the off side of the dog. Dogs don't see colour. They only see shades of black and white and therefore they cannot distinguish between the good guys and the bad guys, only by the actions of the individual and command of their handler. Never get in front of the dog, otherwise it will take you for the offender and may bite. So I am mindful of this when talking to the handler and there is not a problem. I let the handler know that it's at a stalemate at the present and that once the door goes in his dog will be first in and we'll back him up with Bean Bag and OC, so keep the dog on a long leash. Good with that, and back to Col who tells me that we had best start to think about an entry. *Not good, but so be it.*

As I head back to K9 to give him the update, I'm on the radio telling my team to move to the FAP (Final Action Point) and querying with my FC (Field Commander) as to the ETA of Western Power for lights out. With that, I walk up to the K9 handler and start to relay what I had just instructed to my team. As I am talking to the handler, without any warning – nothing – his fucking dog attacks me. From the opposite side of the handler, the dog launches itself across the front of the handler, latching onto my left bicep. Fortunately, with my senses on high alert, being startled by the unexpected and suddenness of the attack, my immediate reflex action is to pull my arm away before the mongrel dog can sink his teeth into me, ripping my overalls as his teeth drag across my arm, breaking a few layers of skin. *What the fuck!* as my right hand moves towards my pistol. But what infuriates me more is the handler.

He chuckles and says, "He doesn't like you much."

"I've got news for your fucking dog. I don't like *him* much," I reply through gritted teeth.

I want to shoot that bastard mongrel right now, but of course I wouldn't, but that is how I am feeling. I am pissed off, because now I have to handover as TC and go get my arm looked at by the ambos. And, wouldn't you know it, while I am having my arm looked at by the ambos on scene, the boys go in.

I am to learn later that this particular dog came from the Prisons K9 unit that work with their emergency response group. They had determined that the dog was psycho and got rid of it, to the WA Police K9 section.

'Sure, we'll take it, we can train it'.

In time, the dog did indeed prove to be a real psycho, attacking its handler in the kennels and ripping the guy's chest apart. Needless to say, the animal is now in doggy heaven. I guess that mongrel dog didn't like his handler as much as he thought it did.

Chapter 5

Officer Down

A call not often heard, thankfully, but it's the one call that runs a chill down your spine,

"Mike 136, urgent, officer down."

A motorcycle cop has been shot. No matter what you are doing, where you are, those words, 'Officer Down' is a call that every cop will hear and every Police Officer will bust their gut to help, just like at the Trigg Riot. There may be calls going out to attend a shop lifter or a stolen bicycle report and no bastard speaks up, but get a call for an 'Officer Down', and they come out of the woodwork. It is the camaraderie of what makes the 'Thin Blue Line'.

I can hear in the voice of Mike 136 that he is hurting, but still, he goes on doing a bloody great job of giving the most important detail: his location: Maylands. *Shit, we're just around the corner on our way to the Police Academy shooting range for practice.* And just by coincidence, we are on the lookout for notorious serial bank robber Brenden Abbott, dubbed by the media as *The Post Card Bandit*. He is known to be in WA at this time. He has plundered just about every state and is enjoying the notoriety of staying one step ahead of the cops and the media limelight cast upon him, almost to the extent of him becoming a modern-day Ned Kelly. Abbott and Co had robbed banks at gun point, dropping in through the roof of banks, shoving the barrel of a shotgun in the faces of tellers who would never be able to work behind the counter of a bank again, so traumatised by the violent threats to 'Blow their head off'.

Now everyone has an Achilles heel, and for Abbott, it is his fuckwit half-brother. He looks up to his big bro and aspires to be just like him. Go figure. I guess that's what makes us cops and them crooks. Anyway, not being the sharpest tool in the shed, this cockhead has been pulled over for a minor traffic breach, puts two and two together and comes up with five: 'I'm being stopped because I am the half-brother of the infamous ...' So, he jumps out of his car, shooting at Mike 136 who cops a 9mm round in the abdomen, the round passing out through the cheek of his arse.

Fortunately, the pistol jams (probably from a 'Limp Wrist' grip) and cockhead isn't able to get another round off at Mike 136 who returns fire from his .38 Smith & Wesson and hits numb nuts right in the stomach and drops him like a sack of shit.

I said this boy isn't too smart: he is using 9mm ball ammo, a full metal jacket projectile which, at close range, can over-penetrate and exit, as it has in this case, probably saving Mike 136's life. The .38 +P Special is a .38 calibre round and, basically, it has the same load as a .357 Magnum round. You can actually fire a .38+P Special from a .357 Magnum revolver. Not good for numb nuts as the projectile enters his gut, the semi-brass jacket peels back like a banana skin assisting in the transferring of kinetic energy to the body ('Blunt Trauma'). The hollow point acts like a parachute and mushrooms, slowing down the projectile and causing a larger internal wound cavity, ripping apart any tissue and bone it passes through and results in the projectile staying within the body. Hence known as a 'non-Exiting' round.

"Oscar eight, VKI."

I nominate our availability and location as my partner and driver, Operator #27, throws our car across the two lanes of traffic as we bounce across the kerb, cutting off cars, scraping the chassis of our Commodore in an uncomfortable screech of metal across concrete. (*Mental note to self – get chassis and wheel rims checked after*).

Patrol bags on the back seat bounce around held in place by the seat belts I toss my coffee mug on the floor in the back, rather than risk wearing its contents. I grab the magnetic blue light between my feet in the foot well and, reaching out the window, I put the blue light on the roof. But #27's superb driving skills are too much for it to stick on the roof and it dangles in the air on the end of the power cord, bouncing around off the passenger side window. I push my hand into the roof to stop my head hitting it, and my feet into the floor well to brace myself into my seat whilst talking to VKI on the radio with the other free hand.

We get a Category A from VKI, which basically means - 'Go Like Fuck': lights and sirens; no stopping at red lights or stop signs. No doubt another yellow peril is coming our way as cars brake, blasting their horns at us and gesturing. #27 is an ex-traffic cop and, although we have all done the advanced driving courses, he is a better driver than me and I am quite happy that he is at the wheel. The radio channel is chaotic, patrols begging to be given Category A, demanding updates, drowned out by their own sirens screaming in the background. The emergency channel operator has his arse hanging out, denying vehicles categories, demanding patrols to comply, all the while trying to coordinate the emergency and doing welfare checks on Mike 136.

There he is on Guildford Road.

#27 pulls up our Commodore just short, turning the wheels so we end up at a forty-five-degree angle, with the engine block offering us some protection. Not knowing if the shooter was still active or not, #27 takes the necessary tactical profile. I can see Mike 136 is on the verge next to his bike holding the two-way radio. Numb nuts is lying on the road just to the rear of his car, a pistol on the road near the driver's door.

#27 and I attend to Mike 136, he's our first priority. *Alive and conscious, fantastic.* Numb nuts is not in a good way as I look at him with a large dark blood stain covering his gut, blood steadily oozing out, but alive. *I'm thinking, I hope it fucking hurts, you cunt* as I walk past him. I feel a smile pull across my face as the first ambulance arrives. Maylands is an inner-city suburb and in direct line of the city's major hospital, Royal Perth. I walk the ambos over towards Mike 136; #27 is with him giving him reassurance. Mike 136 is in pain, his face twisted, fighting the pain off.

Triage dictates numb-nuts is in need of emergency surgery and, when I look again at his gut wound, I know the ambos are right. He has to go to hospital first.

The second ambulance arrives. Mike 136 is happy soon enough, sucking on the green whistle of Penthrane as the ambos tend to his wounds. I recall the time I did an advanced trauma course down at Campbell Barracks and we got to sample what is well-known in medic circles as the 'Green Whistle'. *Great stuff. He won't be feeling a thing.*

I look around. It's like a scene from the TV hit series *Hill Street Blues*, a sea of blue lights and every cop wanting to know if Mike 136 is okay. *Yep! no problem.* He's as high as a kite sucking away on the green whistle as the ambos load him onto the trolley. I have a laugh to myself, I doubt that this many Category A's were authorised by VKI. Good to see our own looking out for each other, even if it meant risking a blister (reprimand). This turn of events gives detectives valuable intel about Abbott, kicking off an operation all around the city and suburbs.

The TRG are on the go for 48 hours. We hit doors of known associates and cheap motels where he was rumoured to be held up. The Ds (Detectives) call us, and we hit a house or motel room and so we go rolling from one door to the next. 'Knock, knock it's the TRG, anybody home?' as the door ram shatters the lock and splinters the door, or a 12-gauge shotgun blasting the door off its hinges. Sooner or later our man will run out of places to hide.

Unknown to us, as we pull into the forecourt of yet another cheap Perth motel along the Great Eastern Highway near the airport, Abbott drives out the other end. Pure arse luck for him. That's how close we come to catching him. Eventually Abbott is caught, in another state. The pressure we put on him and his scaley associates and family is just too much for him to stick around. All thanks to his little half-brother, who recovers to serve a few years in the can. That is how piss-weak our judicial sentencing system is, and society wonders why there's a crime problem. Had he been half smart about the whole thing, he would be paying a traffic fine, not serve a jail sentence and Abbott may still be at large.

Brendon Abbott – "The Post Card Bandit"

Chapter 6

The Informer

Detectives, especially those in the Drug Squad and Armed Robbery Squad, cultivate Confidential Informants (CI's), snitches or fizz as they call them on the Police TV shows. Informants are most likely to be crims themselves or of nefarious backgrounds and character. Only rarely does an average law-abiding citizen become an informant; most members of the public will call 'Crime Stoppers' with information about a crime.

Crims become informers because they want to take the heat off of themselves, save their own skin or get another crook in the shit as a pay-back for some perceived injustice against them. They are not doing it out of a need to do their civic duty. An informant is expected to provide information that promises to be valuable and ongoing. To secure this source, there must be a reward; it could be money, or could be a lesser charge resulting in a lighter sentence. Through a process of vetting, and with the approval of the Commissioner of Police, there are strict protocols that must be observed both for the detective and the crim, including keeping a journal that logs all meetings, the information received and so on.

Relationships of sorts can develop between the officer and the informant as they become familiar with one another's character and rely on each other for their reward in kind. But what happens when this comes to an end, as inevitably it does? A detective moves on, is promoted, transferred, re-assigned or whatever, and can no longer have, or needs to have, dealings with the informant.

The latter may conclude that he has been shafted; his safety blanket has been taken away. Feeling vulnerable, betrayed and angry, he seeks retribution, like in a particular case in which the TRG became involved. The informant demanded a meeting with this said detective. The detective said no; their working relationship is officially over; the informant is no longer of any value. The snitch is furious. His phone calls escalate, from harassment to threats. The detective believes the informer is running with his old crew and back 'on the gear' (drugs). This makes him unpredictable and a risk. It is decided that he should be arrested, if he can be found.

A meet is set up under the guise of resolving the informant's grievances. Phone contact is made, and a time and place agreed on, with certain conditions, stipulated by the informer. *Not a good sign*. It indicated that the trust that had existed between them was long over. There is no way the detective is going to turn up alone. We don't even know what vehicle the informant is driving.

The plan is that the detective is to be at an agreed place and time. A covert vehicle, with an arrest team on board, will casually drive up and, 'gotcha'. We also need a Plan B and a Plan C. The detective will wear a 'wire'. If the informant gets spooked and leaves before we can make the arrest, a marked police vehicle will stage a pseudo traffic stop and make the arrest. I was part of Plan C. If the meet goes ahead and the informant approaches the detective in his vehicle or threatens him, I am his primary protection, hiding in the back of the detective's car.

It's agreed and time to move. Fortunately, for me, the detective's car has a bench seat in the back, so I am able to lay down, obscured from view. I have my G43, a Heckler & Koch, 5.56mm select-fire assault rifle with extendable stock. The calibre can punch through a laminated windscreen or door skin if necessary and still have the 'Stopping' power. With the stock retracted, I can hold the weapon across my chest while lying down and still bring it up to the shoulder quickly to get a sight picture. I also carry my trusted side arm, the HK USP 40-calibre semi-auto pistol which the TRG had transitioned to from the proven Beretta 92F. At the time, the Glock pistol did not have a light rail and someone in their infinite wisdom tried to pass off the S&W Sigma pistol as the weapon of choice, *Bahahaha*!! So, the HK USP it was. I'll say no more about that fiasco.

We pull up at a car park next to the Swan River. Quite scenic really; the covert vehicle will not look out of place around here as it pulls in to make the arrest. The detective gives us all a running commentary as we go, also for the benefit of our TC managing the tactical operation listening in.

"He's not here. I can't see him anywhere. Block, you right in the back?"

"Yeah, no worries," is my response.

In reality, my mind is going through all the 'What if's?'. What if he comes to the passenger's side. What if he comes from the rear. What if he wants to get in the car, with the detective outside of the car? I have to think on my feet (or on my back in this case) and make decisions on the run, and quickly.

"OK, guys, heads up. Looks like our man is here."

The detective shifts nervously in his seat.

"Red Mazda RX 7, parked parallel to the river, facing north."

I know the arrest team will be heading our way now.

"Trying to get you a rego."

If the detective can get the Mazda's registration number, the TC will pass this on to the traffic vehicle, but also get an owner's check run on it, possibly revealing the informant's associates.

We will be clearer about who else we may be dealing with or if the Mazda is stolen. The detective confirms:

"Yep, that's him. Okay, what's he doing? He's walking over to the *Kopper* logs next to the footpath. Looks like he's propping there."

I draw a mental picture of the informant's parked car in relation to where we are and where the covert vehicle will pull up. We are facing toward the river and at a right angle to the informant's Mazda. On his driver's side are the Kopper logs, a footpath running alongside between them and the sparkling Swan River. Behind us is the old East Perth power station, now decommissioned and a canvass for graffiti artists.

The detective gets on the radio. "Yep, guys, he's staying put. Looks like he wants me to go over and see him."

The detective gets out of the car and heads towards the informant.

I'm thinking, *Fuck! Where's the arrest team? OK, I'll stay put and see where this goes.* The conversation between the two doesn't start well and goes downhill quickly. Predetermined signals have been agreed on to be made by the detective if he is feeling threatened. One of the detective's signals is a visual sign, the other, a code word. The adrenalin is really pumping now, and I am starting to consider my options. *Where's the fucking arrest team?*

All at once it happens, I hear the detective's code word. I can tell from the nervous tremble in his voice he is not comfortable. *Shit, I'll go for it myself.* I flip myself over onto my stomach, and with my left hand, grab hold of the door, pulling myself onto my knees in a crouch on the back seat, G43 in my right hand, muzzle down in the foot well. I open the door and kick my legs out to stand up between the door and the B Pillar, offering some protection from the vehicle body and engine block but still able to bring my rifle to bare over the top of the engine block. Shouldering my weapon, stepping out around the open door, I turn to my right. The detective and informant are arguing. The detective steps away, giving the visual distress signal and not wanting to be in the line of fire, stepping well away and making distance from the informant. *Smart move.* I raise the sights of my weapon onto the informant and quickly move forward. I tell myself I as I move, *Mustn't run or I'll miss if I have to take a shot.* If you run, the muzzle will bounce, so you keep your torso rigid by moving from the hips down. *Smooth is fast. Heel toe, heel toe.* It's like having the shits and squeezing the cheeks of your arse together and walking quickly to get to the toilet before you crap your pants. It has the effect of minimising the movement of the torso, stops the rifle bouncing and keeps it parallel to the ground and thereby easier to maintain a sight picture and alignment. In my peripheral, I see the covert vehicle come into the carpark. *Awesome, back-up has arrived.*

I'm shouting at the informant: "Police! Police! Get down! Get down on the ground!"

The boys explode out of the covert vehicle. The informant looks at the detective, then quizzically at the covert vehicle, then the boys and then at me. His face says it all; 'Oh shit, I'm fucked' as he resigns himself to that fact, and lies face down on the ground, arms and legs spread.

Chapter 7

Camp Crusty

The MUA (Maritime Union of Australia) is one very powerful, if not the most powerful, union (apart from the Labor Party) in Australia, controlling what comes in and goes out of the majority of the major stevedoring ports around Australia. And naturally this attracts organised crime gangs. To work on the wharves, to even step foot on the wharves, you have to be a paid-up member of the union: no choice, no membership, no job.

The MUA had a stranglehold over the stevedores, dictating the terms and conditions of work, and they could effectively hold the nation to ransom if not ceded to. Anyone who works on the wharves is called a 'Wharfy' *Very imaginative*. Talk to a Wharfy and they will tell you they work hard and are not paid enough. *Aren't we all?* It is common knowledge that the Wharfy scams every which way they can. One example is that a Wharfy does not even step foot on the wharf for work during their entire roster. Someone would clock on and off for them while the rest of them did ... whatever. Certainly, the Railway Hotel on Tydeman Road, Port Beach, directly across the road from the wharf in North Fremantle, is well patronised by the Wharfy on most days for 'early openers' and the same at the lunch time 'titty show'. Salaries are said to be circa $100K. *Nice work if you can get it.*

Patrick Stevedores and the Howard government are determined to break the MUA's hold on the ports – reduce costs and improve productivity, and as we all know, the Liberal Party is traditionally anti-union as much as unions are anti-Liberal and are Labor supporters.

A quick overview of the politics in play here: the Howard government implements significant industrial relations reform to what has become known as the Workplace Relations Act. This legislation is to allow individual choice in the workplace, thereby reducing the powers of the unions. The Act also introduces individual statutory employment contracts. These are known as Workplace Agreements or AWAs. The union is pissed because the result is that the government and Patrick Stevedores together have effectively watered down the collective bargaining agreement under which the unions operate and thereby surreptitiously weakened the power of the unions on the wharves. The door is open for Patrick's to create redundancies, reduce overtime penalties and entitlements and hire casual employees and non-union labour. In what can only be described as a very clever corporate move, Patrick restructures its business model, whereby essentially non-union labour can be employed by the individual business unit within Patrick's. Each business unit has its own labour hire agreement which is terminable by the individual business unit without notice in circumstances of industrial action. The details of the corporate restructure are not made known to Patrick's employees or the MUA.

On 8 April 1998, Patrick's management dismisses all of its employees; liquidates its assets, becoming technically insolvent, and imposed a lock out at most ports in which it operates with the Howard government fully supporting Patrick's in their action. By the following morning the docks are fully operational with new non-union staff in place.

In Fremantle, the MUA pickets the wharf bringing it to a standstill. As the union and the government enter into litigation, support for the MUA grows from other militant unions such as the powerful CFMEU. The picket lines grow and attract sympathetic support from other unions and the usual anti-establishment, rent-a-crowd professional protestors, the same protestors who would be down the wharf when the US Navy comes to town, when a sacred site is declared on a piece of prime real estate or the government approves uranium mining out in the middle of the desert. The actions of the union's picket is declared illegal whilst due process is being exercised through the industrial courts. For Patrick's, it is business as usual as they bypass the picket lines by smuggling the non-union labour to work on pilot boats from across the harbour and onto the wharf. Every night and early morning the crews are smuggled in and out, and a couple of former TRG guys who had turned their hand to the private security industry are making a 'motzer' running the crews back and forth. Little did I know that I would be working for one of them, 'GT', in the coming years.

'Gino Fast Car', an ex-regiment guy that had transitioned to the TRG, only then to leave to enter into the world of private security, is also spotted sneaking around doing whatever he is doing. In Gauge Roads, the container ships are anchored and not going anywhere. Those that managed to berth before the strike and tied up alongside lay idle, as are the cranes that offload the thousands of shipping containers. The rumour is that Patrick's secretly employed the ADF to operate the wharves as they had all the tickets for the cranes and such, until the new workforce is installed. I guess it only demonstrates the impact of the whole situation as the strike is crippling the supply chains and as such, Australia's trade relations and the economy. The unions know this and hence why they have been allowed to become a force known only unto themselves.

Seeing 'GT' and 'Gino Fast Car' confirmed the rumours to a certain extent, I guess.

The situation escalates with threats being made toward Patrick's executives and the non-union 'Scabs'. The pickets set up camp on Swan Street, turning everyone away, in or out, and are technically trespassing on Patrick's property. The TRG and a number of policing units are mobilised as things begin to get more serious with a court order being granted to remove the picket line off Patrick's property.

Our relationship with the SASR afforded the TRG with a 'Basher' (large green canvas army tent), which is now our billet, set up amongst the shipping containers stacked four high on the wharf. This is where we are camped for the next two weeks, thirty odd members of the TRG, eating, sleeping, farting, eating, sleeping, farting … … you get the idea … welcome to 'Camp Crusty' as it quickly and lovingly becomes known. It is our living, briefing, socialising, sleeping quarters and HQ. 'Camp Crusty' is our home away from home and now the bastion of the TRG where no other man may dare enter.

We soon learn that the MUA has recruited OMCG members, or 'Bikies', to provide extra muscle to intimidate the 'Scabs'. Intel sources reveal that road spikes are being manufactured to throw under the wheels of trucks and whoever may be unfortunate to step on one. Nasty fuckers – pieces of steel wire crossed over and welded together and when thrown on the ground, no matter how they land, a sharp spike is pointing upward waiting to do damage. The government has had enough, and the order comes through to remove the pickets from Patrick's property.

The charter of the TRG is primarily to provide state counter terrorism and a high-risk domestic incident response capability, along with other specialised policing roles. One of these roles is riot control, due mainly to the reason that the TRG is authorised to use chemical agents (tear gas) and this may be used in riot control. We have not done much in the way of training for riots as building a CT capacity is priority and, apart from the infamous Trigg Riot, we had not experienced a riot as such in WA. Because of the criminal element now involved in the Patrick's dispute and the making of weapons (road spikes), it is decided that we are not going to fuck about with these pricks in removing them from Patrick's property. In the middle of the night, we launch our assault on the MUA. Winding our way through the shipping containers as cover, we get as close as we can to the union picket line before breaking cover. In front of us is a six-foot cyclone fence and then some fifty metres of open ground to where the picket is set up. With only our long batons and riot helmets, we scale the fence en-mass.

I hear calls of "Here comes the TRG!"

Someone is well informed!

I look around and see we are in a bit of disarray. No formation or direction. "Form up on me, form up." I yell out, extending my arms as a signal for the guys to form up on me in an extended line. In No Man's Land, we move forward, clearing quite a large expanse of area. The unionists scamper off back to their camp site, with no resistance whatsoever offered in what is an anti-climax to our effort. We push up and stop short of their camp on Swan Street and are met with the usual abuse and heckles from the faceless voices of the unionists from somewhere within the darkness of their camp. We've cleared the illegal picketers from Patrick's property and secure the ground. Gates are padlocked and we return to 'Camp Crusty'.

For the next week, things start to ramp up on both sides. Wives, girlfriends and more rent-a-crowd participants now join the picket lines; their numbers swell. The local populous from around Fremantle provide a ready source of professional protestors ready and willing to fight for a cause, any cause really. BCI (Bureau of Criminal Intelligence) are constantly updating intel on the actions of the unions and some of our guys are out and about doing reconnaissance and site appreciations for our own intel purposes in preparation for the inevitable showdown.

Trunky, the TRG boss, calls me for a chat. Not sure how the

boss got his nickname, maybe it is something to do with his proboscis like nose?

"Block, I want you to be the Tactical Commander for this op. You did well leading the guys the other night."

I am now the incumbent to train up some two hundred plus Police in a large-scale operation to push the union picket line back down Swan Road to Napier Street.

"Okay, boss, sure, thanks. How long before we have to do this?" I quizzed.

"When you're ready," he replied with a wry smile.

No pressure then. In terms of readiness, we are not.

The TRG simply do not have the numbers and I am going to need a hand training the other sections that are also involved in this op. Fortunately, I am aware of guys attached to these other sections that I know personally and whom I have trained in riot control when I was an instructor at the Independent Patrol Group (IPG) where I was attached in a brief interlude before returning to the TRG – hence why I did selection twice – after a five year hiatus at the Police Academy weapons training unit as an instructor.

For the next couple of days, I am flat out like a lizard drinking, coordinating team leaders, training, finding out what riot gear we have on hand, and from there, working out the order of march for the teams, in order of escalation in the use of force should it come to that and constantly reviewing the skills and capabilities of each of the teams. I need to make sure we are all on the same page as far as command-and-control elements, roles and responsibilities, otherwise it can end up it one almighty cluster fuck. And there are plenty of media down at the Police Operations Command Post set up on Tydeman Road that would just have an absolute field day with that. Not to mention that my own personal and professional pride would take a hammering.

All the training is done in disused warehouses on the wharf, out of sight of the unions, media and public. The conditions are far from ideal. The warehouses have become nesting rookeries for what seems like all the pigeons of Fremantle, with mounds of droppings, feathers and dust covering the floor and hundreds of cooing pigeons perched atop of the jarrah beams covering the huge expanse of the roof space of the warehouses. White cobwebs hang in the corners and would look more fitting on the set of a horror movie. Anything metal is encrusted in a salty crust as a result of the moist sea air slowly eating away at it like cancer. Not the healthiest of places I am sure, but as usual, everyone gets on with what needs to be done. The sweetener for all of this is that we are on constant overtime, being that we are living at 'Camp Crusty' on a constant 'call out' status. TRG still has to maintain its CT and domestic response capability.

Time to make the call.

In my assessment, we're as ready as we'll ever be, not much else can be done now. When training up for something like this, there's a psychological factor that must be considered. You reach a crescendo, for want of a better description. Mentally the guys are at their peak, the most prepared they will ever be, but that readiness cannot be held indefinitely and will start to ebb away to a point when it has a negative effect upon performance and frustration can kick in. Then you have to go through a cycle of rebuilding to get back up to that level of preparedness. There's an air of anticipation building; everyone has been holed up at the wharf for the past few weeks and it's now time to go square up with the unions and bikies for the threats and intimidation against people who did not want to be in a union and just wanted to work, but also for the underhand tactics and nasty little tricks like the road spikes. I'm just waiting on Trunky to get back from meeting with the hierarchy to give the thumbs up in what seems like forever to come. No doubt there is legal opinion to be considered, the political fallout and consideration of the unknowing public now involved at the picket line who have sympathised with the cause – all manner of considerations to be made way above my pay grade.

I get a call from the boss, "Block, you have a green light."

You fucking ripper, I am looking forward to this, I am thinking. Not to go do battle, *well okay, maybe a bit of that,* but to put in practice what we have all been training to do – the formations, movement and control. The logistics of it all coordinating some two hundred coppers, commanding guys much more senior to myself, inspectors and senior sergeants, all finally coming together.

In formation, extended lines across Swan Road in six double ranks, we march on the pickets. On approach, I assess the pickets. The wankers have not only got women involved but kids as well. This is a low one in my book; clever strategy on their part, I suppose, but here we are again, kids being used as pawns in a game they know nothing of, let alone playing a willing part.

I bark out the command with as much authority as I could.

"Squaaaads, halt!"

In unison, all the riot teams repeat the call down the ranks. They're doing me proud as well as themselves, looking and hearing very impressive. Crisp blue uniforms, the sun glinting off the visors of the riot helmets. It looks shit hot, and intimidating, as it is supposed to look. The psychological battle has already started. There will be those in the picket having second thoughts. 'This is not what I signed up for. I can't afford to be arrested. I'll lose my job. Nah, fuck that, I'm out of here.'

The teams stop short of the picket line by about ten metres. Over a bullhorn, the OIC of the Fremantle Police Region walks around the pickets reading aloud a proclamation declaring their action unlawful and giving an order to disperse or be forcibly removed. They have fifteen minutes. Whilst this is being read, I move up and down the ranks of riot teams getting thumbs up from the team leaders. The teams are good to go. I speak to

'Moose', who is leading the first rank. No riot gear; dressed in Police blues with standard accoutrements. Their role is to remove the kids and women. Moose is a man mountain, a 'Bricky' (Brick Layer) on his days off. He has paws like a bear, calloused and hard, but a very calm and easy going fellow who has the respect of his troops. I had worked with him in the IPG. The next rank has batons, not to strike with, but to use as leverage, to release the grips of interlocked arms of the picketers. They would work in unison with the first rank, if needed, to apply grip releases and removal techniques on resistant picketers. The rear ranks (TRG) are in full riot gear should it get nasty. By now all the pickets have sat down on the road with chants of "Union rights are everyone's rights," and the standard cry of "Hell no, we won't go."

Fifteen minutes pass and the order comes.

I warn the squads that have been patiently standing by, "Front rank, prepare to advance."

I command Moose's team and immediately Moose and his team snap to attention.

Moose takes control and advances his team up to the seated pickets. My job is to observe the progress of his team and the reaction of the pickets, assessing if I need to call upon reinforcements or even perhaps withdraw the team. Some of the women have their kids sitting on their laps or have their arms interlocked with their kids. It is actually quite upsetting seeing the kids crying and screaming as the big bad Police try and pull them away from their mums. No matter how the guys plead with the mums to cooperate and let them go, they hang on tight, which only makes the kids scream louder, all for the benefit of the media, and this angers me personally. Using CS (tear gas) or Pepper Spray is not an option, partly because of children being involved but also because of the unpredictable 'Fremantle Doctor', a wind that swirls and gusts through the port town. Quite often you can be sitting on the cappuccino strip having a coffee at the famous

'Gino's Café', when the stink of sheep piss wafts past, blown in from the sheep carriers berthed over at North Quay, tainting the taste of the finely roasted beans. *Compliments of the 'Fremantle Doctor'*. The media were getting their dream footage for the evening news.

One by one, Moose and his team pick out targets and remove screaming kids out of the clutches of the mums, the mums themselves and other women. As the team move deeper into the picketers, one by one removing them, I call in the next rank to tackle the more stubborn and determined pickets.

By pushing the tip of the baton from behind, through the arm pit and then rotating the butt over and forward against the upper arm, it works to break the grip of the person, and you transition into a shoulder lock with the baton. You have to be quick and work in tandem with a partner who is ready to restrain the other arm when they let go. Some Police use PPCT (Pressure Point Control Techniques) which is pushing on nerves points like the adenoids or under the soft cartilage of the nose. Some use other methods like the 'Chicken Leg'. All these techniques cause a degree of pain and discomfort, also known as pain compliance techniques – effective on a lot of people, however there are drawbacks. The techniques certainly do not 'look' good from a public perception aspect and secondly if you're not careful, you can injure the party, especially if they have a high pain threshold or are goal-orientated and motivated or are affected by drugs or alcohol. I can just see the news tonight on TV, and it will not be pretty.

Gradually the lines thin and so we begin to push the weakened picket line back by advancing all six ranks on the pickets and forcing them back down Napier Road to a point where a demarcation line had been agreed upon near Tydeman Road. Job done. We experienced more resistance from the mums and kids than we did from any rough, tough 'Wharfy'. But, as it turns out may not be so dumb, when there are plenty of sacrificial lambs, why not get them to do the dirty work for you!

Over the ensuing days, police numbers decrease as does the pickets until finally it is just the TRG holding the fort at 'Camp Crusty' and a skeleton crew of union officials manning their camp. On our last night at 'Camp Crusty', we are called out to attend an 'Out of Control' party up in the hills district of Armadale.

It is like waving a red rag to a bull. Still fired up after a disappointing show by the unions, we hit the road in a convoy of cars for Armadale, a good forty-five-minute drive from Fremantle. It feels good to be free from 'Camp Crusty', and a chance of a bit of action – another house party that had gotten out of control with underage kids drinking and running amuck in the street. I'm impressed. On arrival I can see a car is on its roof and a couple of kids jumping up and down on it. Other kids are just generally being dickheads, shouting and smashing bottles on the road and throwing empty cans and bottles over the backyard fence onto the road from the house where the kids are having the party. Absolutely no respect for the other residents. The street is a mess, and the neighbours are not happy.

A couple of pissed off dads have come outside dressed in their footy shorts and singlets challenging the kids to come on their property just once more and … …

As the anointed Tactical Commander, I form the boys up and we sweep down the street arresting anyone who hung around, and encouraging the dads to go back inside their homes. As we move past the party toward the upturned car, we become the target for the cans and stubbies but, in our riot gear, they bounce off the shields and shatter on the ground. Kids run back inside the house or jump back over the fence into the backyard to escape us. We sweep up and down the street a few times and, satisfied that we have cleared it of 'Kaka's' (juveniles), we turn our attention back to the party house. One has a sense of history repeating itself.

To my surprise, a mum of one of the kids is hosting the party.

Quite open about supplying alcohol to the kids, she is very anti-cop and refuses us entry. When it is explained to mum how many offences she is committing and the consequences, she reluctantly concedes and allows us to enter the house to disperse the little darlings. Remaining outside were ten to fifteen or so TRG and, as we move through the house and into the backyard, the kids jump the back fence, only to be greeted by the boys on the other side providing a welcoming committee for them. There are bodies going back and forth over the fence not knowing which way to go – funny as fuck to see – some even taking refuge by perching on top of the fence.

And of course, we have the media hovering like vultures to get a story. None is forthcoming, so a journo makes up a story and alleges that he is assaulted by Police, by me! *Anything for a good story!*

As we are sweeping up and down the street, I have bought the team back to the start for another sweep. Behind me is a journo, his camera man with his gaffer running out the leads for the camera. I know the journo is there somewhere behind me but is the least of my concerns. As I move around behind the team giving instruction, the camera crew has to back up and in doing so the journo trips up on a kerb. I hear the clattering of him falling over and turn around to see him on his arse, legs and arms flailing around like a tortoise on its back. This is the basis of the alleged assault that is made the next day when I am informed of the complaint by my boss.

"Bring it on, bring it on," is my response.

Not quite the answer the boss was expecting. I am angry.

"Let them make the complaint, boss, and I will see them in court."

One of our guys, 'John Boy', has already been hauled over the coals after footage is released of what appears to be him kicking one of the kids at the party in the head. The saying that 'a picture says a thousand words' is not always the case, especially so when in one dimension and the footage is edited to suit the narrative. The truth of what has actually happened is, one of the kids came leaping over the fence from the backyard with a bottle of booze in his hand. As he jumps to the ground, he falls over and 'John Boy' kicks the bottle out of his hand. *Fair enough, a potential weapon.* I saw the footage and yes, that is what it looks like, a cop kicking a kid in the head. But don't let the truth get in the way of a good story. Speak to ten other TRG that night and they will tell the same account about 'John Boy' kicking the bottle out of this kid's hand because that is what *really* happened.

I guess I was the next in line for the media to have a crack at when the kicking allegation doesn't get to fly. *Trial by media.*

Upon returning to Fremantle, the strike at the wharf fizzled over the next few days and we get the order to return to base. 'Camp Crusty' is packed up and returned to the regiment and the TRG is demobilised back to Police Headquarters where we all submit our overtime claims. I must pass my thanks to the MUA for the O/T (overtime). It was well spent.

*The initial lockout of MUA union strikers
at the entrance to Patrick Stevedores, Napier Road, North Fremantle*

Tactical Response Group advance on the illegal picket line at Patrick Stevedores strike, North Fremantle

Chapter 8

The Job's Fucked

It wasn't too long before we found ourselves back down at the Fremantle wharf, but this time for a completely different reason. A container ship from the eastern states has berthed enroute to some far-off country which was exactly what the stowaways wanted. It is thought that two suspects for a murder in the east have stowed away on this vessel to evade capture and no doubt prison. The ship itself, sailing under a foreign flag and registered in Panama is suspected of being previously involved in nefarious activities. It's a big vessel, with sea containers stacked three high above deck and the same below. We are informed that the TRG is to search all the super structure of the hull. It is a huge task and I think just about everyone from the TRG are here.

It's around nine in the morning and we are parked up alongside the ship at the wharf donning our basic kit, ballistic vest, belt order and pistol. With vessels, we don't talk nautical, too confusing for everyone. It's front, back, left and right. The deck is level zero and anything up is in ascending order, level one, two, three and so on. Below deck is described as minus one, minus two and so on. Easy. We are to search down beyond the lowest level including the engine room and where the propeller shafts enter the structure of the hull. Climbing the gantry, I start to get an appreciation of the size of this vessel and immediately doubt that we will find anyone hiding onboard and if we do it will be by sheer luck.

We breakup into small teams and are given areas to search,

return to the bridge once done to be given the next area to be searched. The superstructure of a ship is like a giant steel rib cage that forms the shape of the hull and sheets of steel form the *skin* of the hull. The hull is compartmentalised to provide strength and reduce the risk of sinking if holed. There are areas that are relatively easy to access and search but when we get right into the bowels of the hull, we find it becomes much, much more difficult. Breaking off from the team, we agree to search compartments individually for expediency and practicality. I found myself stripping off down to my overalls and pistol to gain access into the compartments. Wearing my ballistic vest and belt order made it impossible to squeeze in through the small hatches that gave access. (No "Confined Space" protocols observed in this job). No way a team of guys could fit. Confined space training, what's that? Fall Restraint Harness … don't be silly! The reality is, if we had to observe all the rules and regulations of OH & S, we wouldn't be able to do our job, simple. The pistol is more for a light source than protection. My pistol has a small torch mounted on the underside of the pistol frame under the barrel which is activated on and off by flicking a small switch with a finger. Getting down on my hands and knees crawling along steel beams in dim light, I start to search the compartment. My pistol torch casts shadows across the beams that form the superstructure of the hull. There is no air circulating, and it is very warm, so I am soon sweating. Crawling along, stopping to peer into the dark corners until I have done a circuit and have searched that section, I work my way back to the hatch. I felt like Geppetto inside the stomach of the whale. Crouching down stepping out of the compartment I put all my kit back on and move onto the next area to be searched. Stripping down again and back on my hands and knees crawling along another beam of another section, I come across a discarded blue plastic screw cap from a water bottle. *Someone else has been here before me and it wasn't one of us. Maybe we will find the stowaways after all.*

A shiver runs down my back. If I do find one or both of them, it's going to be interesting as my radio is back with my kit at the hatch.

Back outside, meeting up with the rest of my team, #13 has found where steel plating had been cut and re-welded and we speculated that it was most likely where previous stowaways had been hidden. Our overalls are soaked in sweat as we constantly go from hot to cold, drying out then, only to sweat once more. We all have salt stains around the arm pits and between the shoulder blades from where the sweat has dried out. We need to hydrate big time.

At whatever time it is – must be well after 6pm as it is dark – we have 'smoko' up on the bridge. Tired, thirsty and hungry, no expense has been spared and we are provided with a Macca's burger, fries and a Coke. The food of kings. The Coke is flat, and the burgers are cold by the time we get to eat them.

Murmurs of 'the job is fucked' float in the air as the guys wander off.

"That's just great."

"Thanks, but no thanks."

"I'll give it a miss," and "Thanks all the same."

Back down into the bowels of the ship I go, but this time in company with some guys from Customs who are familiar with searching ships for contraband and such. We are to search down in the engine room and around the prop shafts. They both have gas detectors in a leather case hanging around their necks. Not knowing what they are, I enquire as to their use and I am told that where we are going to search, poisonous fumes are given off that are odourless and, if not detected, fatal. *Well, that's just bloody great. If the salmonella from the Macca burgers don't kill us, the poisonous gases were sure to.*

I've given up on taking my gear on and off, deciding to go 'clean' (belt order only) and just as well, as I am to find that it is stifling hot in the engine room. The heat generated by the huge diesel turbines that turn the screw props, the engines that generate the electricity required to power the vessel, heat exchange engines that suck in sea water to cool the engines, electric motors to drive/power whatever, all within a confined and compartmentalised space combine to effectively create a steel sauna. The checker plate floor is slippery underfoot covered with a mix of oils and sea water.

I carefully work my way around, staying in eye contact with one of the Customs guys for that thumbs down signal *'Get out now'*. No way was I going to end up like a Jew in Auschwitz. The smell of oil, grease and diesel mixed with the sea hangs in the air. Everything is hot to touch, all the machinery is painted in a dull machine green that has been chipped away by years of tools being dropped on them, revealing the gun metal grey primer underneath. Oily handprints streaked across machine cowlings, rags hanging on a piece of wire and asbestos bandage wrapped around hot pipes to insulate against burning whoever forgetfully touches one. My overalls are wet through again with sweat.

We search this vessel for near on twenty hours. Tired, hungry and pretty grotty in our now oil- and sweat-stained, dust-covered overalls, dejected that we had not found the stowaways, we pack up and head back to Police headquarters just as the sun is coming up over the Perth escarpment in the east. After twenty-three hours, given we have to return stores, clean and refurbish all our personal kit and debrief, I head for home driving into the morning sun that is now well above the horizon. I don't remember driving home, I am that knackered physically and mentally.

Over the coming week, I think all of us in the TRG came down with various illnesses ranging from throat infections, eye infections, skin irritations and generally unwell caused through fatigue and breathing in or touching whatever shit that was down in the belly of that cargo ship. It was this sort of things that made the job fucked. Not the lack of OH&S, we accepted that, but the seeming inability of the hierarchy echelons to provide some basics like, decent food and drink. As the saying goes 'an army marches on its stomach'. But had anyone of us been recalled to duty that following day, there would be no hesitation and we would have been straight back into the office willing to do it all again.

I recall doing a bush search when the State Emergency Service (SES) provided the catering. The SES do a great job, I mean no disrespect to them, but they did not appreciate who they were catering for, not on this particular occasion anyway. A platter of sandwiches doesn't cut the mustard and it was demolished in minutes, as was the water – it wasn't enough but most of us carry our own additional food supply as a matter of standard practice.

I like to carry Biltong, a dried salted meat that you can throw in a backpack and it lasts almost forever. I cut small chunks off with my *Spyderco* knife and stick it in the side of my cheek where it would slowly soften and dissolve. A great source of protein. I buy my Biltong from my local butcher, who make it themselves, not this Beef Jerky crap you buy in packets in the supermarket that's soft and tasteless. We managed to convince the powers to be we needed the Police's own Emergency Response Unit, a unit set up for crisis and emergency response management who had all the gear for such operations like natural disasters, industrial accidents and the like and they soon became exclusive caterers to the TRG. But in typical fashion, we are reminded by the hierarchy of the cost to the Police Department and how lucky we are to have access to such. *Boo hoo, suck it up!*

On the next SAR (Search and Rescue) mission, walking out of the bush and down a limestone access track back to the mobile command post, I come upon the Emergency Ops guys at the Command Post with two BBQ's going full tilt with steak and sausages sizzling away and an urn bubbling away, tea, coffee, sugar and juice in plentiful supply. It was a sight to behold. Almost heavenly. That's what the engines of the TRG runs on and we consumed all of it. I don't know how many calories it is but we certainly burn it off as we set off again to continue the search. The SES could not believe the amount of food we went through and put their hand up to say they had no idea but understood our previous whinge at the lack of sustenance. Kudos to the SES for putting their hand up and admitting their bad. For sure it was not to happen again on future ops with the SES supporting.

Chapter 9

Claremont Serial Killer

REDACTED.

Chapter 10

Olympic Flame

The Sydney Olympics is just about upon us and we are now training to provide the security element for the Olympic torch relay that will be run through every state of Australia on its voyage to the opening ceremony of the 27th Olympiad. Of course, we still have our CT commitment and are doing high risk domestic operations along with it, so we are busy little Vegemites.

I am now an Acting Sergeant with my own team.

In preparation for the Olympic Torch Relay Western Australian leg, we have trained for various scenarios whilst escorting the torch bearers from town to town. My team is to provide a C.A.T. (Counterattack Team) vehicle response capability posed by a threat to the Olympic Torch, the torch bearers or the Olympic Flame. Many of the torch bearers are various sporting and entertainment personalities. The torch itself would be a prized trophy for some wanker to steal or extinguish the flame. As back up to the flame being snuffed out, be it by a miscreant or inclement weather, there is a lantern, a gold coach lantern that accompanies the torch throughout the journey to re-ignite the flame should such an event occur. The flame of the lantern is said to be taken from the very flame of the Olympiad itself in Greece. The torch bearers are to be guarded by members of the Police PSCTIU (Protective Services Counter Terrorist Intelligence Unit) or as we call them, 'spies', and their Federal Police counterparts. They will provide a cordon around the torch bearer as they do their run. If attacked, it is their job to protect the runner and the torch and evacuate them to safety. Our job as the C.A.T. is to engage the threat. Ahead of the torch bearer and protection team is a couple of modified Winnebagos that transport the Olympic officials, the lantern, a spare Olympic torch and accredited media. Our vehicle is at the rear of the entourage.

The Olympics is a sponsor's moneymaking paradise. Every available square inch of blank space is an advertising opportunity and MacDonald's (by coincidence), yes of the *Golden Arches* fame, has not missed a trick. The TRG is sponsored by them (I'm sure it's only by coincidence that they also catered for us on the search of that cargo ship in Fremantle). We are being supplied with nice new polo shirts with the TRG emblem emblazoned on one side of the chest and the Golden Arches on the other. Our new baseball caps are the same.

Time came soon enough for the training to be over and the Olympic Torch Relay of the XXVII Olympiad to begin. Travelling through the country towns of the South West of the state, everything is going swimmingly well if not laboriously slow. Every town turned out to greet and wave the torch bearers on their way. Quite a logistical marvel considering the distances being travelled, the number of people involved and the international, federal and state inter-agency cooperation. The weather has been very good for the most part until we arrive in the south west regional town of Bunbury for an overnight stay. The weather turned and for anybody who has been to Bunbury, that makes it an even more miserable town. You drive through Bunbury on your way to the surfing at Yallingup and wineries of Margaret River. But it's not all doom and gloom.

The boss has been given a 'Gold Card' to meet our daily expenses, meals and accommodation and tonight we are treated to a meal at *Josephine's*, an Italian restaurant that is actually quite swanky, for Bunbury, and the food is not half bad. The gold card is copping a hammering: we're all ordering the crayfish mornay or the 500gm grain fed Wagyu steak. Halfway through what is turning out to be a very enjoyable and relaxing evening, or at least it was, the boss gets a call. Some dickhead has barricaded himself in his house, threatening to kill everyone and himself. *How many times have I heard that before!* The locals are in attendance and knowing we are in town have requested our assistance.

'Block, do you mind grabbing your team and heading out to have a look?"

'Actually, yes, I do. I'm quite enjoying my meal, thanks, boss. Can it wait?'

Well, that's what I felt like saying but no way was I going to say that to the boss.

It is only dessert I am going to miss out on anyway and sitting on my arse in a car for eight hours a day moving along at a snail's pace, missing dessert won't go astray.

Grabbing a bunch of equally disappointed guys leaving their sumptuous meals, the only saving grace is the fact we are not paying for them, we head for the siege.

Boof Head is your typical anti-cop, wife bashing, beer swilling, unemployed bogan, who blames everyone else for his predicament and doesn't take any responsibility himself, *looking for yet another handout, no doubt.* And after this is all over, a twenty-eight-day assessment for the psyches to work out that he's not nuts, just a wanker, he'll get yet another leg up.

The local boys have got a cordon in place around the house and the situation is contained. The sergeant-in-charge is a former TRG member, however his guys are not up to taking the next step, if required. No fault of theirs, the 'Regional Response Groups' (RRG), an initiative to provide the country regions with a local 'High Risk' response capability, has not undergone the training required as yet for this sort of incident. I have a chat with the sarge and get the lay of the land from him. I send my guys off to go and join each of the local RRG cops positioned in the cordon around the house to assist and guide them. *Fantastic opportunity to provide 'On the Job' training.* Boof Head in the house has a can of *Zippo* lighter fuel and has dowsed himself down in it and has a cigarette lighter in the other hand threatening to light himself up in tribute of the Olympic Torch. *LMAO, the parody of it all.* Numb nuts has locked all the doors but has left a set of double French doors wide open leading from the lounge room out onto the veranda that surrounds this typical Australian farmhouse-style home, and we have a great line of sight to him. Did I say this guy is not real bright?

Operator #39 and I are with the sarge letting him call the shots. #39 is a very unassuming fellow, nothing striking about him, just gets on with his job, but is very talented, fit and fights like a man possessed. We're here merely to assist as and when requested or necessary; the sarge is in charge, it's his op. The three of us are squatted down behind a 'Super Six' fibro fence listening to this clown.

"I know you pricks are out there. Come any closer and I'll do it and burn the house down."

This goes on for a few hours, back and forth trying to get the guy to come onto the veranda where he could be tackled. Numb Nuts gives himself another squirt of lighter fuel. #39 tells the sarge that he can get onto the veranda if we can distract him. Sounds like a plan and if we can get a couple of others in close, we can rush him. The plan gets the nod from the sarge.

#39 sneaks off and the sarge calls out to Boof Head. As he knows we are out here, I stand up so he can see me which draws his attention over my way as #39 makes it onto the veranda. A couple of the guys have come onto the veranda on the opposite end of the French doors in company with the RRG cops. I step around from behind the fence and move a little closer. Our fella is pacing around in and out from the lounge, fuel and lighter in hand. Sarge is still talking to him and I'm standing in the front yard. Now his attention is divided. Maybe it was all too much for his pee brain to handle, I don't know, but he starts to flick the flint on the lighter.

I yell out to the boys, "Go, go, go."

We all rush in through the French doors whilst this wanker is trying to set himself on fire. One of the local cops takes the initiative and opens up on him with pepper spray (Non-Flammable) and Numb Nuts stands there getting hosed down with OC and still trying to get the lighter to ignite. We all want to move in and grab this prick but the local copper is still emptying the can of OC spray on our man and no one really want to get a dose as well. Everything appears to be happening in slow motion as these things tend to do. I walk around a couch in the lounge across the polished five-inch-wide jarrah floorboards and over to the cop with the pepper spray.

I tell him, "Okay, you can stop now."

I reach across and push his hand down that is holding the can of OC spray, at which point all the boys tackle Boof Head to the ground and cuff him. This guy starts crying like a bitch, begging and pleading to stop the burning effects of the OC spray. Fuck me and he wanted to be a human torch ten seconds ago! Now we have to baby sit this idiot and decontaminate him which is a time consuming and wet process. No PETs here to hand him over to like we did with a girl holed up in a flat in the city one night.

This girl is armed with two big 'fuck off' steak knives and threatening self-harm. Two of the boys with shields and helmets rush her, pinning her up against a wall and I give her a blast of OC in the face. The effects are not instantaneous, and she has the presence of mind to reach over the top of the shields and tries to stab the guys in the head, the blades glancing off their helmets. *The bitch!* After being unceremoniously dumped on the floor and cuffed, we drag her into the kitchen where PET are waiting. I hand her over and one of the PET nurses, who has soaked a few tea towels in the sink, proceeds to wash her face, resulting in her screaming like a stuck pig. I tell the nurse that we have pepper sprayed her and not to rub her eyes as this will further aggravate and promote the effects of the OC. His response to me is by putting a hand up to me in the 'talk to the hand' gesture and says, "I am a trained nurse. I know what I am doing."

I respond in my best Verbal Judo, "Understand that but I am advising you that she has been pepper sprayed … don't rub her eyes."

I had barely got the words out of my mouth and he reaffirms his credentials.

"I am a trained nurse. I know what I'm doing." He dismisses me with a wave of the hand.

Fine, she's in your care and custody now mate, not my responsibility and you are the trained nurse, apparently!

As we gather up our goods and chattels and head for the front door, I can hear the girl scream again as she gets another face wash. I walk off having a bit of a giggle to myself about that one.

2000 Olympic Torch Relay. Sponsored by the 'Golden Arches'

A modified Winnebago in the background used by media, Spare Olympic torch and the Olympic Flame. Harley Davidson's for Police Out Riders

Chapter 11

The Good Times

Fremantle:
Don't get me wrong, I'd had a ball in 'The Job', and met some fantastic people, both in and out of blue. The experiences and training are not something that can be found anywhere, and coppers tend not to realise that and sell themselves short when venturing onto 'civvy' street. I had worked hard and played just as hard.

In the years preceding the Americas Cup Challenge of 1987 in Fremantle, more colloquially known as Freo, the port city was a tired, a historic rundown colonial port with a reputation for a good coffee and fish and chips. There were three nightclubs of note in Freo: Tarantellas, fondly known as Tarantulas, or T&T's Club Sirocco's, also the home of the original Metropolis Night Club, now known as Metro's now in Northbridge of the CBD. All dens of inequity frequented by the criminal low life, prostitutes and cops.

Tarantulas was the type of place that you called the station and told them you were going in for a walk around. If not heard from in five, send in the cavalry. When that place went off, it went off big time, like one of those old western cowboy movies, when the piano stops playing, and the chairs start flying across the bar. If you got called to go to a brawl there, you wouldn't go in without back up. The six cell Maglite torch got a good work out in there.

An old heritage building, the several layers of carpet put down over the many years squelched underfoot from the years of liquids spilt on them, and not all was alcohol. The floorboards were uneven as the foundations had subsided and creaked as you enter the foyer before walking into the bar-cum-nightclub and dance floor. A lot of the old limestone buildings built by the convicts in Freo have seen better days and are in need of dire repair – wood rotting and the limestone walls softening and starting to crumble away – walk in death traps, let alone a OH&S nightmare. But if you were looking for a local crook, this was the place to come. If the crook was not here, someone would know their whereabouts hoping to curry favour with you.

I cut my teeth in Freo as a cop dealing with the crooks.

After finishing an afternoon shift, our crew would often go down to T&T's on a Friday or Saturday night for a beer or three and inevitably end up helping the night shift crew lock up some prick after a brawl (which we did not start, I may add) or having a firm word with one to pull his head in and fuck off. The majority of 'ladies' that drank at T&T's are either single mums twice over or skanks looking for a free drink and an easy fifty for a blow job back of house. Mounted high up on a wall overlooking the dance floor is a cage where the strippers would do their thing. As the booze flowed and the night wore on, a regular would climb up there and do an impromptu strip to the encouragement of the drunken patrons, and it was not always a pretty sight. When the US Navy visited Freo on R&R, all the 'Wharf Rats' *(Skanks, whores, sluts, you get the idea)* come out and try to attract an American sailor who is 'young, dumb and full of cum' and has a wad of US dollars to splurge, get pissed and get rid of his dirty water.

Club Sirocco was just around the corner from the Freo cop shop. If we had 'Choir Practice', Sirocco's was our next stop before heading home or to the Federal Hotel for 'Early Openers'. Every now and then the owner of the club would hold a 'Cops Night'. Ten dollars entry, beer was half price for a jug and spirits were cheap. Needless to say, it was well-patronised by the Fremantle constabulary and CIB. The strippers were usually better quality than T&T's and not so many crooks to contend with, but it was a favourite with the Japanese fishing trawler crews and so also frequented by the classier 'Wharf Rats'. They pretty much kept to themselves as we did. The local Ds would often be seen having a quiet chat with one of the ladies of the night or the club owner, no doubt getting the drum on some crook about a drug deal or armed holdup.

With a fairly steady arrest rate, I got to know some of the detectives at Fremantle. In those days, the CIB had a 'Duty Driver' where a uniform guy would basically be their taxi driver for the week of night shift driving them around from club to club socialising with the licensees, crooks and locals. It was a great opportunity to learn the trade craft of being a detective and learn about how crooks operate and how to deal with them.

Metropolis Night Club was the upmarket night spot of Fremantle, I guess. A lot of local businessmen, bank staff and shop owners would drink and socialise there on a Friday night after work and so would the higher profile crims of the time, like a former Golden Gloves Champion, who also likes the marching powder, being his eventual downfall. Many feared him because of his propensity to violence. It is said that he was responsible for many more rapes than he had been charged for, but the victims were just too shit scared to come forward for fear of retribution. The reality is, he is just another shithead, a big fish in a little pond.

There was the international drug dealer said to be the Perth link to the Barlow and Chambers Thai drug smuggling case. He was mad as a cut snake. Both were involved in the infamous Fremantle Prison Riot where I found myself doing the high-risk escorts to and from the Central Law Courts during the trials when I was at TRG. During the prison riot trial, he appeared in the dock stark naked. He has a set of balls like a stud ram. Maybe that's why he was such an angry little man. He smeared his own shit on the holding cell walls at the central law courts to piss off the prison guards, but he also pissed of his fellow inmates and they gave him a flogging for it. You've got to love prison justice. He would yell out all sorts of obscenities to pedestrians from inside the prison truck as it made its way down St George's Terrace on the return run to Casuarina prison after the day's presentation of evidence to the court, yelling out that he could smell some young pretty secretary's cunt standing at a bus stop.

As we were in police uniform escorting the prison trucks, the public would look at us expecting us to do something about it. We would cringe and melt into our seats with embarrassment. What could we do? *Absolutely nothing!* He is serving life – he doesn't give a fuck. Then there is the multiple rapist, for whom a well-known local television journo gets the hots and is caught passing notes to him during the prison riot trial and we gladly remove her from the court. She started visiting him in prison, so the story goes, go figure. Some women are attracted to the bad boy types and he certainly fitted the mould.

Another crim, a druggy, and an armed robber merchant, whom I had the pleasure of 'Taking Out' when I was in the TRG after he had been fingered for yet another stick up during a brief stint of freedom. He was lying down on the grass in a park in Mosman Park, dozing in the warm afternoon sun. UCOs had been keeping obs on him until we arrived and we more or less walked up to him and arrested him. At least he didn't have to far to go back to his second home, Fremantle Prison.

They had all the journos fooled and half the jury I'm sure as well. Walking into the specially designed secure dock seated behind smash proof Perspex glass screens, they would appear dressed in shirt, tie and trousers, and clean shaven. One had taken to wearing glasses and a woollen cardigan, trying to look demure and intelligent, guilty only of 'minor' offences attributed to coming from a rough upbringing. They aren't fooling any of the constabulary, however. They are vicious, sadistic bastards. I locked up a lot of crooks during my time in Freo, and I have some good pinches. House breakers, unlawful wounding, sell and supply, rape and manslaughter.

Choir Practice:

Choir Practice is a well-known institution in policing, or at least it was. It's code for a 'piss up' after work, generally at the end of an afternoon shift before starting a new roster cycle. The call would be put out over the local radio channel that was not monitored or recorded by VKI, announcing that Choir Practice is on. The 'Church' was located down on the banks of the Swan River in North Fremantle, now the site of the WA Water Police base. A police van would turn up, after collecting the order for 'verses and chapters', which was code for the order of stubbies and cans to be consumed, the favourites being Emu, Swan and VB. (*The boutique brews and foreign import beers had not hit the market as yet*).

Choir Practice is a great way to unwind, relax, talk bullshit and blow off steam without fear of being overheard or seen or hassled by some interfering 'do good' citizen or ladder-climbing career officer. There is no rank or file; everyone speaks freely, sergeant *and* constable. Once the beers had been downed, the sergeants would generally head home to their respective families whilst us young bucks, all revved up, would head to a club. 'Staffies' is a tradition whereby once a club is closed, the patrons kicked out and doors locked, we continued on drinking with the manager and bar staff, usually on the tab (free). As the first rays of light cracked the horizon, occasionally we would kick on to 'Early Openers' at the 'local', opening at six am, perfect timing as 'Staffies' would just be winding up. Opening at 6am attracts a gathering of local alcoholics and the homeless down and outs who would crawl out from whatever hole they were sleeping in to prop up the bar and continue their constant state of inebriation.

A few times we would head to the Raffles Hotel for the 'titty' show, counter lunch and Kevin 'Bloody' Wilson at midday, sobering up until the start of the next afternoon shift at 1600 hours. There were some big nights had, punch-ons with local crooks and liaisons made with respectable young ladies whom we had managed to impress somehow during the course of the night. I recall going to a 'Cops Night' at Sirocco's during my first stint at TRG, such was the reputation guaranteeing a good night. Not recalling much about the night before and feeling a bit worse for wear, I turned up at the TRG office for work the following day only to see my offsider 'GT' with lumps and bruises all over his forehead. I couldn't help but laugh but became more concerned when he started laughing at me and pointing to my head. Then the memory of the night before the morning after. We'd had a headbutting competition and, by all accounts, we had given it everything and it was declared a draw. Now we sported the bruising and lumps across our foreheads.

*Sirocco's Night Club and Tarantella Night Club.
Dens of Iniquity.*

Dining-In Night

At the TRG, there is a standing tradition with the Australian Special Air Service Regiment (SASR) that we are invited to dine with the Regiment at Campbell Barracks, Swanbourne, usually an annual event – though some years were missed due to global and political issues – a black-tie evening, silver service and hosted by the RSM (Regiment Sergeant Major) with Warrant Officers and Commanding Officer sometimes in attendance. It's a night to be revered by all, to be invited by the elite of the Australian Special Forces and share their company and camaraderie, a time to absorb the history of the SASR, read the plaques and inscriptions around the walls adorned by pictures of conquests and seized enemy memorabilia and the close ties that bring us together on this splendid night.

The evening commences with pre-dinner drinks before being called to take our seats at the dining table. The RSM commences proceeding with a toast to the Queen, which is saluted with charged glasses of port. Our Officer in Charge (OIC) reciprocates with a complimenting toast to the Commanding Officer of the SASR, acknowledged with recharged glasses. The compliment returned toasting the OIC of TRG and then the RSM SASR (Our Host). We work our way through a three-course meal befitting a Michelin star restaurant. During the courses, there are more toasts and traditions to be observed and glasses raised to absent friends, apologies, fallen comrades and the more humorous toasts as the port courses its way through our veins. Bloody hard work standing up and sitting down through the evening as I think just about everyone finds a reason to raise their glass for some noteworthy toast.

'Dining In' nights were made even more relevant and poignant given that the TRG has former SASR troopers serving with us and SASR veterans since retired. Many I have the pleasure to serve with during my time in the TRG and to be trained by them during their service defending Australia.

Retiring to the bar to continue good conversation over generous pouring's of your chosen spirit, diner jackets are soon discarded over the backs of chairs and ties are loosened.

I recall my last 'Dining in Night'. I went out in style – found on the sports oval which doubles as the LZ (Landing Zone) for the Black Hawk helicopter, where I had aimlessly wandered off to in a state of total inebriation. I was fucking hammered. Guided back up to the mess by the boys and dutifully put on the bus for the returning trip home. Enroute, the contents of my stomach stripped the paint off the side of the bus as I puked the night's ingestion of spirits out through the window. I recall my wife greeting the lads at the front door thanking them for returning me home safely, whilst I heaved up the last contents of my stomach in the driveway. Touch Rugby the next morning at work was not as energetic as it normally is, but like everyone who was at the Dining In night, I was there. Failing show and it would not be something no one would be allowed to forget.

and

NOW

A well-travelled passport. Australian Customs & Immigration upon my re-entry into Australia "Holidays, Sir?" with a knowing smile as I was waved on through.

Chapter 12

IRAQ

I think anyone you talk to can remember 9/11 and what they were doing on that history defining day. For me, my usual morning ritual of having my morning cup of tea, I wandered into the lounge dressed only in my undies. My wife was staring at the TV gob smacked. My immediate reaction was 'Bullshit', and I asked her if it was a trailer for a new movie. From there I stood glued to the news for the best part of the morning when my phone starting ringing.

The state manager of CHUBB security (guarding) was on the other end and her first question was: had I seen the news, and we need to meet. For me this was an opportunity to make a real impact on the local security industry which I had been finding a hard nut to crack. I was about to find out why.

Following the meeting, I presented a proposal that I felt addressed her needs, as outlined in respect of upskilling the company's terrorism response capability. Of course, they wanted the world; they wanted to provide their clients with highly trained personnel, by yesterday (as always) – and here's the clincher – for rock-bottom dollar. Don't they all? Instantly it told me they were not serious. It was about the brand and KPI's. I walked away. It was a sad indictment on the state of the private security industry in Western Australia. And not much has changed. In time, I was to get my chance, but not in Australia.

The second Iraq war is now in its third year: it's 2005.

For the past few years since I left 'The Job', I have been running my own security training company, at home, delivering training in the tools of my former profession. It is doing my head in with the poor standard of guards being employed in the industry, the amateur companies operating in the industry, and the so called 'Instructors' doing the training. It is certainly a case of 'Pay peanuts and you get monkeys working'. *Fuck me*, I am thinking. *I am better off going back in the cops* when a SASR mate of mine tells me that there are jobs going for tactical coppers in Iraq, so it's decided. I put my hand up for the gig.

'Operation Iraqi Freedom' is in full swing. Suicide bombings are common place and at least sixty headless bodies are being dragged out of the Tigris River each week. I arrive at BIAP (Baghdad International Airport) via Jordan and Dubai to run the gauntlet of 'Route Irish', a twelve-kilometre-long stretch of road that is the most dangerous road in the world (at this time). It's the main road in and out of BIAP to the Green Zone.

It makes sense that the insurgents concentrate all their efforts on this one stretch of road. A PSD (Personal Security Detail) team had already lost lives on Route Irish in a now infamous ambush and the IED's are becoming more ingenious and treacherous. The US has given code names to all the MSR's (Main Supply Routes), many associated with State side, such as MSR Los Angeles and MSR Cleveland. Route Irish obviously links the strong Irish heritage of US ancestry, or perhaps because it was the only road in and out of BIAP.

The level of security around Baghdad is identified by the colour for each zone. The Green Zone was supposed to be a relatively 'safe' de-militarised zone, the CBD of Baghdad. It is where all the US, Coalition and Iraqi Government offices are located. Someone must have forgotten to tell the insurgents, however, as they are still launching their mortars into Baghdad and going about their business with regular monotony, targeted assassinations, VBIED & PBIED's (Vehicle Borne/Person Borne Improvised Explosive Devices) and shootings.

The International Zone (IZ) was the next concentric ring where most the PMSC's (Private Military/Security Companies) are located along with the general populous of Baghdad.

The Red Zone is everything and everyone else beyond the IZ, a no man's land if you will.

Like a lot of tactical coppers, I have picked up a gig as a Training Advisor under contract to the US DoD (Department of Defence). Our charter is to train the new Iraqi Police Force. We muster at Camp Victory in the Green Zone, where I am issued the famous AK-47, a 9mm Glock, Ballistic Vest and Helmet, which I give away as a bad joke as it looked more like a WWII Japanese helmet. We spend a couple of days in the Green Zone waiting to deploy to 'Camp Num', as it is known in the south, but for now billeted at Camp Victory.

A visit to the PX (military supply store) is mandatory, a lolly shop for PMSC's – it sells everything from sim cards to weapon slings. I get the latest statement in fashion, a pair of Wiley X goggles for a quarter of the price anywhere else and a shemagh, along with a few other bits and pieces. Some guys go to great expense buying accessories to trick up their AK until it looks more like a M4 (standard US military issue assault rifle).

We eat at the US mess facilities, compliments of our US DoD ID's we have been issued. There is everything you could wish for at these mess halls. Pizza Hut, Burger King, Wendy's, kosher and halal, hot and cold selections. I line up with US soldiers with their rifles slung over their shoulders amassed at a former palace of Saddam, all facilitated by Halliburton and KBR (compliments of Mr Cheney & Mr Bush Snr). It is as amazing as it is surreal to see. Here I am in a war zone in the Middle East, thousands of kilometres from the US and I can go to Burger King. The logistics operation in itself is staggering but I don't think that's what George Bush Jr meant when he said "Shock & Awe" in his announcement preceding the invasion of Iraq.

Talk about a small world. Here I am, standing in line waiting to get in and get a feed, when two faces walk out that I immediately recognise. Two of my former 'oppo's from the TRG back home, whom I hadn't seen since I had left five years back.

"We're not here; you haven't seen us," was their opening line, with large grins on their faces.

Turns out they are moonlighting whilst on annual leave, a practice frowned upon by my old employer and most of the world's law enforcement agencies and military alike. In the early years of the Iraq conflict, the SASR blacklisted many PMSC's from headhunting their guys as so many had left, attracted by the real prospect of putting into practice what they trained so hard for and paid considerably a lot more money. In time, the ADF reviewed the remuneration of its special forces to retain the years of experience they had invested in so heavily, and now that the worlds SF's (SASR, 22SAS, Delta, SEALS, Green Beret) are in the theatre of war, many have returned to the fold. It had been the same with the tactical TRGs of the world's police forces and here are two guys flying under the radar as many police agencies are not so forgiving.

Route Irish is the main access road running between the Green Zone and BIAP. VCP's (Vehicle Check Points) are controlled by the US military. BIAP is the main transit hub in and out of Iraq, a supply route for Iraq and beyond. With military convoys constantly travelling the route, in-country procedure required non-military personnel to stay well clear of their convoys and not approach on the risk of being perceived as a threat and getting brassed up (shot at). The rear vehicle of a convoy has a big red and white sign hanging off the back, written in Arabic and English, warning of such foolish behaviour and the consequences thereof.

Intel is constantly updated, vital to the security of the US and Coalition Forces and reassessed dependent upon insurgent activity in the various AO's (Areas of Operation) of Iraq. PMSC's however are generally not privy to this intel so there are things going on we don't know about, or we would be provided with updates after the fact.

On one fatal day, a PSD (Personal Security Detail) team in low profile soft skin vehicles had propped on Route Irish behind a military convoy, obeying the 'Fuck Off, Stay Away' sign. The military convoy had stopped for reasons known only to themselves. Unfortunately, the decision to go to plan B came too late for the PSD team. Insurgents had already been on their Thuraya mobiles spreading the word that coalition military and civilian security contractors had stopped on Route Irish. A van had positioned itself opposite on the inbound road and simply opened fire. From there, it pretty much went to shit for the PSD team. The on-board video camera capturing the murder of private security contractors went viral.

Most SOP's (Standard Operating Procedures) considered 30 seconds the limit to prop in any one location. For them, however, minutes had passed and, sadly, they paid the ultimate price. For PMSC's to operate overt, up armoured, or low profile is a matter of choice for some, dependent on the area of operation, budget, the services they are providing, experience, their appetite for risk and the client's requirements. As with everything, there is a trade-off.

Up armoured, you have more protection from SAF (Small Arms Fire) and generally carry more firepower, but you stick out like dog's balls to the insurgents. Low profile, you blend with the local traffic but have limited firepower, and are in a vehicle that offers little protection from SAF and IED's. Guys hang ballistic vests over the back of their seat or on the inside of the doors for protection.

The guys whacked on Route Irish were operating in low profile vehicles but wearing tactical order which immediately gives away who and what you are. I knew guys who would sport beards, stain their skin with tea bags and wear a *kaffiyeh* (traditional Arabic head dress) to try and look like a local, or at least not stand out as much. PMSC's would regularly change vehicles, changing number plates and other modifications to make them look 'local'. This just goes to demonstrate the level of counter-intelligence conducted by insurgents and the efforts PMSC's would take to thwart them.

Along Route Irish there are blast barriers or 'T Walls' offering protection from SAF and IED's in the event of an ambush. The blast barriers are made from reinforced concrete, three or four feet thick and lowered into place by crane. One day, a vigilant US soldier noticed something different about one particular section of a 'T-wall' and, on closer inspection, discovered it was in fact made from plaster and had an IED concealed inside.

The insurgents are getting help from foreign terror groups – you can speculate from whom – and are improving their tactics all the time.

Route Irish is driven as fast as safely possible. In fact, that is how you drive everywhere in Iraq: the less time on the road, the better are your chances of survival. The insurgents are pretty much guaranteed whoever they shoot at or attempt to blow up is a legitimate target in their book. *Welcome to Iraq.*

Driving at speed is for good reason: it makes it hard for insurgents to get a good sight picture. Varying your speed makes it difficult for insurgents to time a command initiated IED detonation.

We are getting around in up armoured, V8 Land Rover Discovery 4WDs. I like the fact we have good all-round vision, height and firepower. Being a V8 means we have the speed and power that is normally lost with the additional weight-gain in up armoured vehicles. The doors and windows are modified to have firing ports, allowing you to push the muzzle of your AK out past the door skin to return fire if needed. There is a light machine gun in the back, a PKM, which is the soviet version of the GPMG (General Purpose Machine Gun), link fed and a heavier longer barrel version of the AK-47. The rear gunner can also release smoke, tear gas and distractions in the event of a contact or getting overrun by locals if spotted by locals in a traffic jam. Higher ground clearance also means we can go off road, like mounting kerbs and foot paths to get around traffic jams or the local driver blissfully unaware of 3 tons of 4WD bearing down on them at speed. In time, tactics are to change as the theatre we are operating in is also evolving.

VCP's are manned by Iraqi police, military and sometimes coalition forces conducting overwatch. We display our company ID and hold up our own credentials in the window to get waved through, with little or no hindrance. As the Iraqi Government took more control of its country's destiny, I realise that the Iraqi military and police were flexing their muscle as the Coalition took a step back. PSD convoys are now being stopped and demands for money being made. *The Iraqi version of capitalism.* So PMSC's take their chances going low profile and hope they will get waved on through along with the rest of the traffic at a VCP. Others carry cash to pay off the military or police. It's just how it is.

Occurring more frequently now were VCP's being operated by insurgents in the absence of any of the authorities being in situ. Wearing stolen uniforms, they masquerade as police or Iraqi military, hoping to get lucky. VCP's are a pain in the arse for PSD teams, especially those who are still waiting for their licenses to come through from the MoI (Ministry of Interior). It can take months, even longer, to get your license to operate legally in Iraq as a PMSC. The MoI is notoriously slow and inefficient. If you hassle them, they just dismiss you with a wave of the hand and your paperwork goes to the bottom of the pile, unless you're prepared to grease the wheels. It is common practice for PMSC's to have a local 'fixer' who liaises with the MoI and pay the required 'fee' to expedite your paperwork. It seems everyone wants a slice of the billions of dollars being pumped into the country by the US government. Many of the PMSC's made their own ID's while waiting for the official one – the job has to get done – and the more official it looked the better. Thankfully, the Iraqi police and military don't appear to know the difference.

Hitting 140km/h on MSR Tampa, we are having a pretty good run, managing to miss the mad morning rush of locals heading to the markets and the endless cues of drivers lined up for fuel.

"RV 6, RV 6, water pump station, say again, pump station. Green side, green side," is the call from our TL.

"Roger that." Acknowledgements come from the team members.

Everyone makes a mental note and acknowledges the RV (Rendezvous Point), giving each other the nod and thumbs up signal. Some of the guys have gone to the trouble of buying themselves a Magellan and plot the RV. I double check and look around for other landmarks to reference with the nominated RV. It would be meaningless anyway in another two kilometres as a new RV is nominated and, with this and constant commentary about traffic conditions, potential ambush sites, sus vehicles and people, the chat is hectic over our comms and everyone is busy. RVs are nominated in case our vehicle becomes disabled and we have to evac the immediate area, meaning run like fuck, hide and hopefully meet up later at the pre-designated RV. That was the theory anyway. Hopefully I will never have to put that theory to the test.

Five up in our Disco (Land Drover Discovery), it is cluttered with gear – personal and operational: grab bags and kit. Each team member has his own area of responsibility and arcs of fire. Everything rattles and vibrates. To talk, you have to shout above the engine and road noise. It is pretty cosy inside the B6 (level of vehicle armour) and not all of us are issued with headset communications. Suddenly we slow, brake hard left and zigzag across the lanes. I grab one of the straps hanging from a door pillar as the 4WD lurches across the road.

Another call by the TL over the comms. "Overpass, overpass," yells our driver, confirming the TL's call.

Insurgents will wait on an overpass or bridge for a likely target to come along and try and drop a grenade on you or launch a RPG (Rocket Propelled Grenade). The idea is to try and keep the insurgents guessing where we may pop out as we pass from underneath. My eyes are darting everywhere, checking approaching vehicles. Does it match the description of a suspect VBIED given out at the mornings briefing? A local standing on the side of the road … are they holding a Thuraya (used for command-initiated detonation of an IED) and looking for tell-tale signs of a potential roadside bomb, all at 140km/h. My adrenalin is at a constant high. The first few times, it is like a high you have never experienced. You get a hard on that Linda Love Lace cannot conquer. My senses are buzzing, all working overtime.

I had experienced something similar in the TRG but not to this climatic level. We do two-month rotations and, at the end of a rotation, I find myself mentally fucked from the intensity, and am ready to go home for a break. I guess you would only understand if you experience it yourself.

Num, the base where I work, is a former military camp of the old Ba'ath regime located south of Baghdad. It's a perfect training ground with half completed multi-storey buildings left abandoned and spread out over a twenty-something square kilometre area. There is a contingent of US Marines and Iraqi National Army on the base and ourselves. We number about thirty, supplemented by a six-man DynCorp (US) team who just dropped by one day and stayed. Recruited from all over Iraq, we train goat-herders, farmers, former police of the old regime, and Kurds, to be the new Police Force of Iraq. Many of the recruits are illiterate, in poor health, physically weak and of unknown and questionable backgrounds. The Kurds are hated by the Iraqi' yet they are determined to contribute for the greater good. I find them capable and willing. Each recruit is paid around US$700 per month. That is a world of wealth for the average sheep shagger.

The recruits from the old Ba'ath regime are mainly the officers and are placed in charge of a squadron, platoon or battalion, depending on their rank, but old habits die hard. They are lazy, unfit, conniving and all sporting the Saddam look-alike moustache. And brass. They love wearing their medals and insignias on their uniform. Image is everything to them. Frequently I find them skulking around in an abandoned room smoking and staying well out of the way of anything that remotely resembles work. They want all the praise and recognition but aren't prepared to earn it. No matter how hard I try to get them involved with the 'hearts & mind' psychological bullshit, they aren't about to change anytime soon.

On this particular day, an officer marches a recruit up to me telling me, "This man … he is shiiiiiit."

Like a schoolboy, the recruit is looking down at the ground, embarrassed to be berated by the officer. I look at him and, to my surprise, I see he has fair hair and blue eyes.

I ask the officer to explain.

"He is shiiiiiit, he is Kurd," I am told in his heavy Iraqi accent.

Now this explains this officer's disgust in the recruit. The fact he is a Kurd from the north of Iraq, who are despised by Iraqis from the south. I tell the officer how it is: his duty to his country is to mentor the troops and to lead by example; how he should be proud of anyone, Kurd or Iraqi, who wants to fight for the new Iraq and Freedom. *Rah, rah, rah* but I didn't get too carried away like some did on base who would carry on about truth, justice and the warrior spirit. It is very important for Arabs not to lose face or be embarrassed, but it was taking all my effort not to give this officer an arse kicking. I can understand the Kurds wanting their own autonomous state, already known as Kurdistan, with a capital city, Erbil. And a very good job they are doing of running it, I might add. Iraq on the other hand (Baghdad) is in a shit state if I am to cite a difference between the two.

I am getting my quarters in shape, blacking out the window, taping up the frame to keep the ever-encroaching Iraqi sand out and making a set of shelves out of a wrecked bed to put my personal belongings on. Everything has a fine coating of dust settled on it. The shower and dunny is another story which I attack with bottles of bleach, disinfectant, rubber gloves and a scrubbing brush before even considering using either, and even then wearing thongs in the shower. No longer a biological hazard, it has taken me two days to get them clean and fit for use. God knows what it was that stained the tile grout. The water for the shower is stored tank water and you don't need to turn on the hot tap. Sitting stagnant in plastic tanks, the Iraqi sun is enough to heat the water for the shower. I never swallow any of the water, open my eyes or let water get in my ears and constantly blow my nose out to prevent any bugs in the water getting in via one of my orifices. Guys suffered from the dilapidating 'Jardia' which is a parasite that attacks the stomach. The little bastard can be found in faeces and is blown around in the wind, settling wherever. This is reinforced when I witnessed our recruits shitting in the derelict buildings we are using for their training. Perfectly decent 'Port-a-Loos' outside but they preferred their traditional ways of taking a dump.

It is important to have some R&R from the sand, shit and recruits. 'Dubbs', an ex-2RAR Commando, and I set about fixing up the former 'wet mess'. Fashioned from wooden ammo boxes, frames from broken bunk beds and mattresses, we put together a couple of couches, a bar, a stand for the TV and stereo and, of course, taking pride of place, the Aussie flag mounted on the back wall. We are able to get *Toborg* beer and meat from a South African security team embedded at another camp not far away and, on the last Thursday of each month, we have 'Hadji' night where we have a BBQ, watch 'Team America' (*Fuck Yeah*) on the DVD and generally talk shit and blow off steam. Friday is 'Holy Day' in the Middle East which means the day off for ourselves, with some admin work required where necessary and an opportunity to enjoy time away from the recruits.

On one such 'Hadji' night, we invited the contingent of US Marines based at Camp Num to join us, feeling somewhat guilty that they were in lines doing 'hard tac' (tents, camp beds and MRE's) and we had air conditioning, a wet mess, TV and all the mod cons in comparison. As the evening wears on and the piss flows, the Yanks, not used to full strength beer, fired up. A game of darts soon deteriorated when a K-Bar combat knife replaces a dart, only to be replaced by a tomahawk thrown by one of the Seppo's, which completely obliterates the dart board. *Game over!* And so was the night pretty much. I could never work out why anyone would carry a tomahawk to a BBQ. *Go figure*. We never did invite them back for another 'Hadji' night.

One particular night, I am in my room and I hear the call come over the two-way radio. "Stand to. Stand to!" summoning everyone to the parade ground.

Grabbing my AK off the floor next to my bed, I double over to where there must be at least five hundred recruits massed and our guys tooled up taking up positions around them. Maybe I should have grabbed the GPMG I also had in my room. I am quickly filled in on the story that the recruits are refusing to return to their dormitories because they feel they are being unfairly treated and it looks like things are going pear-shaped. The incumbent Program Manager (PM) is going through the diplomatic process of trying to resolve their grievances.

"We want water like you," says their spokesman.

We all hold up our plastic water bottles. The same water bottles they get.

"We drink the same as you. Have you ever been given fresh bottled water every day?"

No, of course they hadn't. End of that argument.

"The food is shiiiiiit."

Most had never had three cooked meals served to them every day. Lucky if they get one meal a day. Next problem.

"Our room no good," is the next complaint.

"You sleep on a bed, with blankets and pillows in air-conditioned rooms," is the reply from our boss.

For many, it was a case of sleeping under the stars on a blanket in the desert with the goats before they came to Camp Num.

A big American red neck working with us hocks out a big wad of chewing tobacco onto the ground and, in his long southern drawl says, 'Goddamn this shit, there's only one thing they understand." He walks up to the closest recruit and drops him on the spot with his riot baton.

"OK, meesta, we go to beds now. Alahkoom Salam," is the immediate response from the representative speaking on behalf of the recruits.

And with that the recruits dutifully wander back to their respective dorms. Now I don't condone what the Yank did, be it right or wrong, this was the kind of rule the Iraqis understood; it was how Saddam had ruled for decades. And the fact is, we are sadly outnumbered, and the matter needed to be put to bed immediately (excuse the pun). Like every other third world country that has had a taste of western democracy, they want everything, and they want it yesterday, and who could blame them, but they are just not ready or capable to manage it.

On recruitment day, literally thousands turn up at the gates to Camp Num hoping to be picked. Others are recruited in Baghdad, by arrangement. They would produce their *Gencia*, their name is ticked off the list from Baghdad and in they come, the balance made up of those who turn up on the day. The *Gencia* is the Iraqi ID card, a cheap, laminated piece of green paper with the relevant details of the individual, photo ID (all in Arabic) and of poor print quality. Most are in a shit state and verifying their ID is a laborious process of collecting biometrics and sending them off to the MoI for vetting back in Baghdad. By the time clearances come back, training is almost over anyway. The trouble is we simply did not and could not trust the Baghdad vetting or the *Gencia* provided and, as it turned out, we are totally justified. A couple of brothers catch our attention.

They have branded themselves with cigarette lighters and a hot knife engraving Arabic symbols into their arms, and slashing the back of their necks with razor blades. We found drugs – speed most likely. One had a keyring fob with the picture of terrorist leader Muqtada al-Sadr who was leading the insurgency movement through the south. The self-harming and scarring is common in extremist groups. Drugs are often supplied to a would-be martyr to help them overcome any second thoughts they may have before offering themselves to Allah. With them high on speed, we end up fighting them until we could physically restrain them both. Questioning is futile so we throw them into a vehicle and drive out to the main entrance of Camp Num and they are shown the gate. Hopefully they had not learnt too much about us and 'OpSec' (Operational Security) had not been compromised.

It is a sobering realisation that we are providing the recruits with weapons and live ammo with which to train and at any moment any one of them could turn their weapon on us. After this incident, I notice more guys wearing their ballistic vests when out on the range training the recruits, in spite of the blazing sun. Everyone carries their Glock pistol, that is just SOPs, but not all carry their AK with them. I carry mine everywhere. Call me paranoid. The AK-47, the Kalashnikov 7.62mm is the Glock of assault rifles. It's simple in design, robust, reasonably accurate, easy to maintain and almost fuckwit proof. Now I know why the child soldiers of Rwanda and just about every other army in the third world is armed with them or a version thereof. I have the AK S model (S for Skladnoy – a folding stock) which makes it an assault weapon ideal for room combat or, with the stock extended, a field weapon. This is the same model Saddam had gold-plated for himself. He had others silver-plated and given to his favourite generals and his sons. I recall this Jarpy, six-foot, blond curly hair and blue eyes, driving from Baghdad to our base, by himself, in a little white Suzuki jap crap car, talk about trying not to stand out, just to show us a silver-plated AK with ivory stock and pistol grip he had picked up on the black market. The cleaning rod was bent but, apart from that, it was pretty impressive, I must say. Then he drove back to Baghdad that same day, I assume the big fella made it back safely.

As reliable as the AK was, a gun is only as good as the nut behind the butt. For most, our recruits seem to have absolutely no idea of muzzle direction or awareness. Whether it is room combat or fire-and-movement drills, their muzzles went everywhere, into each other's backs, everywhere but toward the enemy.

"Point your gun at the enemy or you kill your friend," I tell them, pointing my finger in the direction of the targets.

"Insha Allah, is the reply – Insha Allah meaning "God willing." *Fuck me, that is the answer for everything in Iraq.* It is God's will if they shoot their mate in the back, it is God's will if they die today, it is God's will if I win fucking lotto. *Don't they want to live?* I retort back, looking at the interpreter for some reassurance.

"Insha Allah," is his reply.

Fucking hell, no wonder this country is in such a shit state. There is no way we are about to change centuries of religious culture in months, years or in a generation, and who are we to try anyway?

One particular Iraqi, who works as a translator for us, had lived in the UK and is very well educated having attended university in London. He has refused to work under the Ba'ath regime so, when an opportunity to work for the new Iraq government came along, he jumped at the chance. Everyone knows him as 'The Professor'. Now this is from an Iraqi national and his words resonated with me. He estimates it will take at least three generations of Iraqi to be trained and educated to western standards before there would be a generation that would be of any worth. (Ten years, I think it was when the US and Coalition Forces pulled out. Now look at the place!!)

Recruit training is twelve-plus hours a day, six days a week with only Fridays, Holy Day, as their one day off and recruit training is long and arduous. In the opinion of our PM, the uprising in the parade ground is as a result of the recruits being fatigued, separated from their families and living in close quarters, so he decides to give them a break with a weekend off. Much to the disagreement of us all, the PM lets the recruits go home, hoping this would placate them after the boil over. We consider this will compromise our OpSec and every single one (1,500 plus or minus) of them will have to be searched and vetted again on return, notwithstanding the disruption to the training schedule it will pose, but we could work around that. Nonetheless, the decision has been made. But before they can go, we will do a full inspection of their dormitories. Room by room, we inspect the dormitories, the beds have to be made, uniforms hung in the lockers and floors swept. Going into the shower and toilets is, well a shit fight, literally, no other word for it. It is Middle Eastern culture not to wipe your arse with toilet paper like westerners do. Nor do they sit on a toilet – they squat over a hole like a drop box and use water to wash their clacker. One way is to use a bidet, you may have seen them in your hotel room on holidays. Some have a hose attachment on the wall next to the toilet bowl or push a button and water squirts up your bum to wash it. *Drip dry, I guess?* Or as in this case, they use their water bottle to splash water onto their arse to wash it, which might explain as to why they were carrying on about their water bottles at their protest. The set up in the ablutions area is a row of a half a dozen or so open drop boxes. No tapped or running water. They use their water bottles to wash their arse with and then go and shove the empty bottle down the toilet. The end result is shit splattering and trodden everywhere and the shitters bunged up with empty water bottles. We are looking at the floor floating in shit. It is disgusting: the smell is unbelievable. How long the toilets have been in this state is anybody's guess. We have enough health issues to contend with already amongst the recruits such as gum disease and other ailments caused by poor nutrition, hygiene and general poor health. We tell them that they cannot go home until the toilets are clean. And attack the shitters they did, with gusto, their arms down the toilets and shit up to their elbows they go about unblocking the toilets. Now they can wash the shit down the toilets and clean the floors.

Using a toilet brush, they scrub around the toilets and they eventually get the place reasonably clean. But they still have the hand basins to clean, which they proceed to use the same toilet brushes they use to scrub the shitters with. And do you think we can stop them or try to explain to them not to use the toilet brushes? In the end, I just said, "Go ... finish, go home."

They look at us with big smiles and state, "Jayyid Jaddan," meaning that they had done well, in Arabic.

"Yes, yes, Jayyid, now go home."

As one of the recruits proceeds to wash his face and arms in the sink, and cups his hands to have a drink from a tap he has just scrubbed with the toilet brush, dry retching, I have to turn away before I puke. I have to remind myself we are training nomadic tribesman who have never seen a toilet and are illiterate. They use sand to flick up onto the shit on their arse and rub off when it dries to clean their backsides. Now I've used eucalyptus leaves with mixed success, but never sand. Clearly, we have a long way to go. It never occurred to me that they would need lessons in how to clean a shitter 1-on-1, like we did for brushing their teeth. Most of the recruits have never seen a toothbrush or know what toothpaste is or the concept of cleaning teeth. I am glad I didn't get lumbered with that job when I saw the gum disease suffered by many who pass out unconscious during training due to the pain of their rotting gums.

Iraq is a place of stark contrasts of abject poverty and exorbitant wealth – again, typical in many third world countries. Poverty and power.

I am about to run the gauntlet of Route Irish again to exfil back to Australia for a four-week break and I have been hanging around for a few days at the company's villa in the IZ waiting for the word. I have done the tourist thing and visited the famous Victory Arch (the crossed swords leading to the national sports stadium). Every PSD team gets a pic here. Not today. We are warned off that it is not safe for us, as a sniper is running around taking pot shots. A team photo would have to wait, so I settle for one of the crossed swords from our 4WD.

As it was, I needed to go to the US Embassy to sort some paperwork out and off we go to the US embassy at the Republican Palace, one of Saddam's favourites he had spread around Baghdad. After all the usual security protocols, I was allowed into the embassy. It is opulence to another level – marble statues hand carved by artisans from Europe, stone and parquetry floors and gold leaf embossed fixtures. Huge chandeliers hang from hand painted dome ceilings. And that is what has been left behind, rescued by coalition forces before the looters had a chance to make off with the rest of it. The craftsmanship is superb, and I only get to see a small part of it. I am told that all of Saddam's palaces were much the same, the craftsman imported from the venetians. In fact, the complex at Camp Num was built by a construction company from Yugoslavia, and Saddam had refused to pay them, so it was 'down tools brothers, we're out of here'. Yet, outside of Baghdad, you can easily find poverty: mud brick homes and subsistence living; no power or running water or sewerage. Iraqis continue living much the same way they had for centuries.

Green Light! We have a green light to get to the airport.

After hurtling down Route Irish once more, going through the VCP's, we pull up out the front of the departure terminal at BIAP.

Now it is time for me to sanitise myself of Iraq: load bearing vest, ballistic vest, assault order, helmet, mags, knife, comms and finally my weapons. Packing all this gear into a kit bag for storage until my return in-country and throwing the kit bag back into the back of the 4WD, I change out of my fatigues and into 'civvy's'. We did all this out the front of the departure terminal. I felt quite naked, an unusual feeling not having the reassurance of my AK, a feeling short-lived when I remind myself, *I'm going home*. When you get the green light to get to BIAP, it's a mad rush to get there before the threat level changes and getting through security can be horrendously slow. If the status changes, flights can be cancelled and, if it's a serious threat, the airport can be locked down resulting in missing your flight and more days kicking around Baghdad. Most guys use their Carry-On bag in-country as a Go-Bag (a 24-hour emergency evacuation kit) and, after two months, you forget what you have in which bag. No need to take a suitcase as you really don't need much in the way of clothing. Fatigues for everyday wear and a set of civvy's to wear when flying in and out. You can leave a fair bit of personal kit like toiletries, towel and runners at the camp for when you come back, travelling as light as you can, leaving room for the duty-free booze at the Dubai airport. I manage to get everything into my 'Day-Bag', and I carry my laptop in a pelican hard case. I have to wonder, every time I go through Dubai Airport, at all the contractors who are still wearing their 5.11 pants and Altana boots trying to look 'Tact-a-cool'. The last thing I want to look like is a contractor from Iraq.

Everyone gives themselves a pat down, making sure they have removed the remnants of Iraq from their person and that you have the two most important items, your passport and your plane ticket. With that confirmed, picking up my day bag I make my way into the terminal to negotiate three security checks. It is refreshing to walk into the air conditioning of the terminal hall after the oppressive heat of Baghdad.

Check Point One – Ticket & Passport to establish your purpose for being at BIAP.

Check Point Two – baggage search and finally,

Check Point Three - Check In, passport and pat down.

I just got through Number Two when Macca, an Aussie, the guy next to me in line, fails check point number two. Security have opened his carry on and have searched it. Macca has forgotten he has a 30-round loaded AK mag in his bag.

I look at him like 'You idiot'.

He looks at me and we look back at the security guard and Macca just says with a silly grin on his face, "Ooops."

Assuming he's in the shit, we're expecting to get bounced off the flight, at best. Nonchalantly, the security guard looks at the mag and throws it over their shoulder into a box full of the fucking things, next to the box full of cigarette lighters. Cool, we walk quickly into the terminal proper and I am on my way to going home, via an overnight stop in Dubai.

Left: Prep'd & Ready for the Route Irish run to BIAP 2005

Right: Mementoes of Operation Iraqi Freedom

B6 'Up Armoured' V8 Land Rover Discovery or 'Disco' with Run Flat tyres. NOTE: Gun ports cut out in door skins.

Chapter 13

Guinea

Contracts come and contracts go. They can have the rug pulled out from under them at any time or you can be bumped off to make way for someone's mate. I suffered the latter. No dramas. I picked up on the training I had been keeping alive on my rotations off back home and picked up some extra work doing defensive driver training for a mate whose company had a contract with oil and gas services company Schlumberger. The gigs were four-day junkets to Dubai, in the United Arab Emirates (UAE). Two days of teaching road craft and the rest was R&R and travelling.

Most of the guys did this gig during their four days off from 'The Job'. It was crème on top of their regular salary. However, this particular gig was a bit left of centre. Guinea. Guess that's why he asked me if I wanted to go! Guinea is on the coast of West Africa, bordered by Sierra Leone, Cote D'Ivoire and Liberia to the south and where Mt Nimba, a UNESCO World Heritage listed jungle is located, the proposed site for a new iron ore mine. Mt Nimba rises some 1000 metres plus and holds huge deposits of iron ore.

Guinea is yet another African state that has been raped and pillaged over the centuries by the colonial masters. I think everyone has had a go at it at some time or another, leaving their legacy, which is evident in the architectural style of buildings and influence on the locals. French is the national language and Islam and Christianity the two main religions. The art of classic patisserie is one legacy the French had left behind that everyone, including myself, enjoy on a daily basis: Croissants and crusty French bread rolls. President Conde has been on his death bed for near on two years and the military are basically running the country. Conakry, its capital, is in a shit state of repair. With the departure of their colonisers, the infrastructure has been left to ruin with no industry to really speak of – a melting pot just right for extremism to come in and take over, offering martyrdom to the disenchanted youth of the country. When multinational *BHP Billiton* offers the President a new deep-water port, a railway line across the country and all the other economic benefits that come from mining, of course he is going to say yes, regardless of whatever UN treaty had been agreed upon previously.

I flew into Conakry after a seven-hour layover in Paris via Dubai from Australia and something like twenty-three hours of travelling. I felt buggered, my fatigue compounded by the stifling heat of Guinea. The airport is in chaos but their system, if you can call it that, seems to work, somehow, albeit very slowly. It was mayhem, a sea of people waving passports, papers and cash above their heads jostling for attention and service. Flights are being called out over the p.a. system and names of passengers called out above the noise in French, then English and I think is Arabic, by the ground staff of the various airlines.

After handing across my passport with the mandatory 'fee' inside, customs and immigration duly stamp my passport and I am allowed to enter Guinea. Met by a local driver holding a placard with my name on it, I am herded outside the terminal and swamped by local taxi drivers touting for business while locals grab at my bag, all clambering for the possibility of an earn.

My brief here is to deliver Defensive Driver training to the local employees of a mining consortium, a skill I had learnt in the Police Advanced Car Course for Police Tactical Operators. The overarching objective of this gig is to achieve zero harm by the reduction of vehicle crashes within its own work force but also minimise that impact upon the wider community of Guinea. It's a simple fact: more people commute via land transport than any other form of transport, therefore it stands to reason more people will have car crashes. Another simple fact is many developing, and third world countries don't have any kind of mandatory driver training to qualify getting a driver's license. Just pay the fee and off you go.

I recall this particular gentleman once telling me in his self-assessment that he was an excellent driver. In his thick Arabic accent, he tells me, "Saeed, I am for excellent driver, I never have crash."

I enquire further. "So how often do you drive?"

His reply: "I drive many, many times."

Okay, I am thinking but still doubtful. "And what car do you drive?"

To my amusement, his answer was one I was not expecting.

"I drive donkey, I never crash, I am excellent driver."

Very proud of himself he was. LMFAO. (*Laugh my fucking arse off.*)

Placing my faith in the hands of my local driver, we head out into the chaos and madness of cars, trucks, buses and other assorted two-wheeled and four-legged transport that is the main highway into the city. The constant blaring of car horns, blasts from of a Policeman's whistle in an attempt to direct traffic and drivers shouting at one another, we wind our way to town, the air-conditioner working overtime to push out cold air against the heat of the day. *Would help if my driver wound his window up.*

Perched on the concrete median running down the middle of the highway, local traders set up shop, selling anything from tooth paste to live chickens hanging by their feet from the stalls. There is no courtesy of an indicator to change lane; no giving way or filtering, but plenty of hand gestures and sounding of horns. But again, it all seemed to work. Ahead, I see that the traffic is now oncoming, straight towards us, in the same fucking lane. I grip the back rest of the seat in front of me. *Wise choice you made, Block, sitting in the back.* I subconsciously check my seat belt. Someone has decided that this is now two-way traffic. Now we have the same chaos but going in both directions. This happens in Conakry, I am told, the idea being to ease the traffic congestion, as needed. *Bloody hell look at the size of that pothole. That's not a pothole, it's a crater.* Such is the sad state of repairs needed on the main highway of Conakry, and there are plenty of them about. My driver casually swerves around it and weaves his way down the highway between potholes, traffic and street traders trying to push all manner of wares through the window. Finally, we make into the capital for an overnight at the Novotel. Tomorrow I am to fly to Nzerekore and then drive on to Mt Nimba, near the Liberia/Sierra Leone border.

Enduring a similar ride back to the airport the next morning, and feeling not much better from a less than average sleep as you do when jet lagged, I am bundled through the domestic departures lounge to a waiting twin prop Antonov that looked like it has seen its best days during World War II. *Okay, two engines, that's a good sign.* Not so sure about the ground crew kicking the tyres though. *No worries, mate, she'll be right.*

Getting our boarding call, I climb the steps at the rear of the plane. Business class is at the rear; up front is cattle class. And who said these countries are backward? I could see locals carrying on board hands of bananas, even a live chicken in a woven basket. *Nah that can't be a goat, surely? Yes, it fucking is.* Surreal, just like out of a black and white Humphrey Bogart movie. Well, I guess that is why they call it 'cattle class'. In business class, we have the luxury of a table that drops down from the side on which to rest my complimentary can of warm coke, *mmm yummy,* and something I had not experienced before, except on trains – passengers opposite sitting facing you.

There is a handful of westerners travelling on the flight and, just my luck, I get this pom who knows everything ... been there, done that and wouldn't shut the fuck up talking about it. *He should be wearing a t-shirt with FIGJAM on it.* 'Oh, lucky me,' I think, wincing a smile at him. Waiting to take off, sweat starts to bead on everyone's skin when next thing we hear the pilot – Russian, of course – coming down the aisle, bellowing at non-plussed passengers, climbing over luggage, the goat and chickens, telling everyone to get off the plane, but in a not so polite manner. But hey, who's going to argue with a charged up Russian captain of the plane your about to fly in?

He pulls down on the lever of the door adjacent to my seat and gives it a good kick to open and the steps drop down to the ground with a thud. At least now I know how to open it in an emergency if I need to.

He yells, "Get off, off, fucking off you all."

Of course, business class is ushered off first and told to stand under the wing. The shade from the wing offered more relief than the struggling air-con on the plane. *Where's that pom?* I am not standing anywhere near him as I manoeuvre under the wing. As it turns out, the ground crew have not loaded the plane correctly and it had to be reloaded.

After half an hour or so, it is getting pretty hot in the midday heat and the shade of the plane's wing has been defeated by the sun's fingering rays. I look to the east and ominous grey storm clouds are building. Eventually we board the plane again, the company chambray shirt now clinging to my skin, real nice against the vinyl seat promoting yet more sweat as I sit leaning forward in my seat, plucking my shirt away from my skin in an attempt to get some air circulating around my body.

Lurching into the sky with the drone of the twin prop engines, the pom is flapping his chops about whatever, and I think even the twin props are trying their best to drown out his incessant dribble. I switch off. The condensation belching out of the vents above the portholes finally starts to have some cooling effect as we climb. I lean out from my seat and looked down the aisle. Just to top it all off, a woman is setting up a cooking stove in the aisle and she intends lighting the fucking thing. *You have got to be shitting me.* Chickens, bananas and goat … well, I suppose she has all the ingredients. Thankfully one of the trolley dollies is on to it.

I shake my head in disbelief, lean back and settle into my seat as we fly straight into the grey storm clouds I had seen building while we had waited underneath our planes wing on the tarmac. Now, over the years, I have flown in all manner of aircraft – helicopters, single and twin-engine light aircraft, as well as commercial carriers – and I thought the landing at BIAP is pretty harrowing. In Iraq, the pilot puts the plane into a steep corkscrew-like descent on final approach. This is to avoid SAF (Small Arms Fire) and RPG (Rocket Propelled Grenade) and most of the pilots are Russian. As it turns out, they are the only ones who have this experience in flying commercial liners in war zones or are mad enough to do it. But this flight was about to take the cake. The plane yawed and rolled and, at one stage, I don't know how many hundreds of feet we must have dropped hitting an air pocket. I left my stomach up there somewhere. But the electrical storm was as amazing as it was scary, and I think I am about to meet my maker this day. I seriously think about calling my wife to tell her I love her and to tell the kids the same.

After two hours of the most nerve-wracking flight I have ever experienced, and even the pom had shut up, we land at Nzerekore Airport in a cross wind and rain sheers. The Antonov approached side on to the runway and we hit the deck and skip and bounce along the dirt runway. We made it. I take my hat off to Russian pilots and certainly do not begrudge them a shot of vodka if they so feel the need – they earn every drop of it.

"Mr Simon? My name is Stevon and I am your driver. Please this way," I'm greeted by a local, whose English is actually pretty good.

"G'day, Steve. Is this ours?" I reply, pointing as we walk up to a standard mine issue, white Toyota Landcruiser personnel carrier. Throwing my bag in the back, I climb in and start to get my bearings. The back door opens and we're joined by a crew from UNESCO.

"Mind if we get a ride with you. Our driver hasn't turned up. We're going to Mt Nimba as well."

Someone is obviously well informed, I think.

Handshakes and hellos all around and intros are done. Peta was probably in her mid-30s, Australian and from Perth. *Small world.* Jackie was more my speed, with an accent I can't work out. I look out the rear to see the Antonov heading back into the clouds, bolts of lightning silhouetting its polished aluminium frame against the grey backdrop of the storm. *Got to love them Russian pilots.*

As we wind our way along the dirt road, the bush gradually turns to jungle and the elevation slowly climbs as we head to Nzerekore township. I learn that Jackie and Peta are here to look at the proposed mine site and the impact it will have on the environment. Mt Nimba is home to one of the few remaining chimpanzee troops in the region, as well as other endangered species of flora and fauna. I feel a pang of guilt when told this. But I am not about to get involved in the politics of it all.

I ask my terp (interpreter), "Steve mate, how far to Nzerekore?"

"Two hours, Mr Simon," is his reply.

Time to sit back and take in the jungle.

Nzerekore is the only town in the region of Mt Nimba and sits on the savannah at the base of the mountain range. Peta and Jackie are getting off at Nzerekore and we are to pick up Michel, the French chef for the Nimba camp. *Oo La La.* As it turns out, a chef he is not. More like a Fitter and Turner, fits into pots and turns it into shit.

"Nice to meet you girls. Take care. Bye," we bid the girls farewell.

The girls enter, what I am reliably told by Stevon, a hotel that looks more like a dodgy backpacker's hotel. We are at Nzerekore, a trading post for provedores and the surrounding local villages. It is the only place where some basic mechanical repairs, parts, fuel and supplies can be sourced other than Conakry. Mt Nimba is still another two-hour drive away through the jungle.

Michel appears. In his best English with a strong French accent, he introduces himself and asks if we can help load the stores and, of course, we oblige as we load up the Landcruiser. Everything is in cans and bottles. *Fair enough*, I think, *less chance of food poisoning*.

Driving on, I can see that, in the wet season, these roads must become impassable even for 4WDs. The ground is soft just from the afternoon seasonal rain. We pass through a couple of small villages. A United Nations emblem is emblazoned on a wall next to a hand-pumped water well. The hand pump is in ill repair but hey, the kids are enjoying playing on it. The UN hadn't left any spare parts for the pump or taught any of the villagers how to maintain it. *Onya UN*.

We begin to climb Mt Nimba, winding our way up through the lush green jungle. Water has cut deep channels into the dirt road. Stevon engages 4WD and we continue our ascent of Mt Nimba. In parts, the temperature drops as the jungle canopy closes over and the light is filtered out, instantly warming again as the canopy opens up once more. The camp is situated probably around 750 metres up Mt Nimba, and serves as a base for the exploration and surveying teams drilling to assay the ore content of Mt Nimba.

Over the next couple of weeks, I am to train up some twenty local nationals employed as drivers for the exploration and drilling teams. The driving route I decide to take to conduct training is the only road up and down Mt Nimba to Nzerekore as this was the bulk of their driving work. Train as you play, the old saying goes, and it was on one particular run returning from Nzerekore that I have my first encounter with the Guinean authorities.

We have left Nzerekore behind and are on the mountain savannah, approaching the climb back up Nimba. Up ahead the road is pretty straight, and a vehicle is coming toward us. As it draws nearer, I realise it is not the camber of the road but how the vehicle is loaded – it's an over laden bus. On top of the bus is all manner of brightly multi-coloured hessian bags strapped to the roof and, perched on top of that, are yet more passengers, villagers taking their wares to Nzerekore to trade. The bus is so overloaded and top heavy it is leaning precariously to one side.

"Stop, stop," I tell my student driver.

While he did his best to bring the 4WD to a gentle stop, not grinding the gears and staying on his side of the road, given he is under the added pressure of having the driver trainer onboard, I grab my camera. A great photo opportunity and one for the album. I jump out onto the road, waving at the bus. As it pulls up, locals hang out of the windows waving; everyone up top are waving. I show them my camera and they all continue to smile and wave, so I take that as the nod of approval as the bus comes to a stop. Clicking away on the camera, I notice one of the passengers step out from the rear of the bus. *No wait, that's a soldier and he's carrying an AK47*. He walks over and starts remonstrating at me, obviously not a happy camper. Maybe the passengers were waving me off, not welcoming me. *Too late now.*

He grabs for my camera. *Hey! Steady on there, fella, what's your fucking problem?* I'm thinking as I pull away, clutching my camera. He rattles something off in French.

Wasted on me, I turn to look at Stevon to translate. "What is his fucking problem?"

"Mr Simon, he wants your camera."

"No way … no fucking way," I tell Stevon.

I turn back to look at the soldier and realise that I am wasting my time. His pupils are like pin pricks; he is sweating profusely and agitated, white saliva flecking the corners of his mouth. This guy is stoned on something. Next thing he sticks the muzzle of his AK-47 up my nose. *Fucking prick*, my anger boils up inside.

I cautiously look down along the barrel to the working parts and he's got his finger on the fucking trigger. Down the side of the receiver group, I can see the long lever of the safety catch is off. *Shit*. My brain immediately dumps a chemical cocktail into my body making ready for whatever decision I make next. As a tactical police operator, I had learnt how to control this and use it to my advantage. *Controlled aggression*. You've heard the saying, 'The mist rolled in and the eyes rolled back.' If you've ever seen a pub fight, there's a flurry of wild punches with maybe one or two actually connecting and results in both adversaries physically exhausted afterwards. That's uncontrolled aggression, caused by the sudden dump of adrenalin, endorphins and fear, wasted in five seconds. But you can learn how to use it to your advantage. Time slows, senses heighten, increase of clarity of the situation at hand. *Okay, Block, no sudden movements, this guy is out of his tree, don't eyeball him. Don't show your fear. Control your breathing, control your speech.*

Everything becomes very clear and precise, my thinking sharp.

Talking out the corner of my mouth back at Stevon sitting in the 4WD, I tell him, "Okay, Steve mate, tell him I have no pictures of him."

Stevon is giving it to the soldier big time. Even in French I could tell that Stevon is as pissed off at this clown as much as I am.

"It's okay, Steve. Steady, mate, just calm down."

Stevon backs off, realising our friend has the AK47 and the advantage.

"Tell him I did not take a picture of him. I will show him the camera."

Slowly and deliberately, I scroll my thumb across the screen, so it is blank then turn it around to the soldier. He seemed to acknowledge that his ugly mug was not on the camera. *Dumb prick!* I think. He rattles off again at Stevon.

"Mr Simon, he wants money."

Yeah, I bet he fucking does, the wanker! At least now the muzzle of his AK47 has dropped but his finger is still on the trigger. A lack of weapon discipline and poor training – both can be fatal for me.

"Steve mate, get a couple of cans of coke out of the esky, mate. Tell him I have no money."

I could hear the guys scrambling around inside the Landcruiser.

"Slowly," I added, not wanting to cause our soldier friend any concern. The esky is in the very back of the Landcruiser strapped down with a seat belt.

"Mr Simon, Mr Simon."

Stevon didn't have to say anything else as he leaned out through the passenger window with two cans of coke. My eyes not leaving the AK47, I reach back and take the two cans and pass them slowly forward to the soldier. With a grunt and nod of approval he accepts the coke and saunters his way back to the bus, AK casually swinging by his side. The safety catch is probably still on the fire select position.

Sitting back in the passenger seat, the fear hit me. My hands start shaking and I got that cold shiver at the realisation of what could have been. I feel mentally fucked. All quite natural, the bi-product of mental duress caused in such situations. Stevon is apologising to me big time and cursing the soldier in a mix of Anglo-French. Stevon explains to me that the soldiers have not been paid in months and, with the President gravely ill and the country left to be run by the corrupt generals, the soldiers are running amok, stealing, standing over villagers, using intimidation and violence. The intimation came that the village women were also being raped. This is my first of two encounters with the authorities I am to have, the next back in Conakry.

Peta and Jackie arrived at our camp earlier in the day and are sitting in the shade outside the kitchen when I rock up after finishing training the last of my drivers. I sit down and learn that the mining of Mt Nimba is going to be pretty devastating to the whole ecology of the reserve. I find them both very interesting to talk to and it is obvious they are both passionate about their jobs and I don't blame them. I'm all for saving endangered animals and environments. Don't get me wrong ... I am not a 'Greenie' by any means, but this struck a chord with me. Stevon and Michel join the group, as does Johann, the resident medic, OH&S officer and snake catcher in his spare time. Johann, a South African, has all manner of snakes of various sizes and colours – some are in glass terrariums, others in sacks and plastic bins. He relates to me that he captures and releases them later as the locals will kill them. Funny enough, by sheer coincidence as we are talking about snakes, the chimpanzees and other species on Mt Nimba, Jackie points up and lets out a sort of yelp. There, coiled up on a branch in the tree above us is a snake bathing in the afternoon warmth of the sun. We all look up. It is beautiful. Black with a red underbelly and quite big, even when it is coiled up.

"Is that a python, Johann?" I enquire, pointing and immediately doubting my own question. I have never seen a black and red python, not even on Nat Geo.

Johann begs us all to be quiet and not look at it, explaining if the locals see it they will kill it. "Simon, help me catch it – it's a Spitting Cobra," he says.

"Help you catch it? Fuck off! I will help the locals kill it," I exclaim.

"No, no. I have a snake pole. I will go get it and we'll catch and release it in the jungle."

Johann, rejecting my idea, rushes off to get his snake catcher's paraphernalia.

We continue gawking at the cobra, blissfully unaware of the concern it is creating. Wisely, we all move our chairs out from under the tree. Johann returns with his snake catcher's pole, the type with the hook on the end, and a calico sack. He hands me a pair of safety glasses and tells me to put them on. I'm thinking, *why the fuck am I doing this*, and *what about Michel the chef, his meals have been shit?*

Cautiously I ask, "Ahh, Johann, why the glasses, mate?"

"It can spit up to 3 metres," he excitedly explains, preparing his snake catching gear. "Get the venom in your eyes and it can blind you."

He is loving this. Johann is in his element. He wants me to hold the sack open and he will drop the cobra into it. I hold the sack open and look at the distance between my hands.

"No fucking way, mate. I'm not doing that," I tell Johann, much to his surprise. "I'll help you, but I am not holding that fucking bag for you."

Michel hands me a plastic storage box he has fetched from the dry store. "Here, use this, Simone." He smiles as he passes the box to me. Maybe Michel had heard me complaining about his cooking and this is pay back.

"Okay, Johann, you catch the fucking thing and put it in the box, and I'll whack the lid on."

Johann is already climbing the tree. The cobra is not amused at being disturbed from his snooze in the late afternoon sun. Next thing, the fucking thing falls and lands on the pavement under the tree. Everyone takes a step backwards. Johann is into it, manoeuvring his catching pole around its tail to drag it away.

"Simon, put the box over here."

I obediently follow, watching the cobra as it stands up, opening its hood and displaying its anger at being woken up and some

Jarpy poking it with a stick. All it wants is to be left alone.

It is an amazing specimen, its black scales and the amazing pattern of its red belly glinting in the afternoon light. Then it spits at me. It launches its venom, recoiling and letting fire with a stream, hitting me fair and square in the face. Johann skillfully coaxes the snake toward the box; lifts its long body up to the lip of the box; encourages the cobra into the box. I am holding the lid to the box like a shield. No fucking way am I going to get bitten, not here where there is no helo medivac.

I quickly slam the lid down and jump back, holding my arms up as if to give the 'all clear' signal. By the end of capturing this bloody snake, Johann and myself are drenched in venom. The serpent has had a go at both of us. I cannot believe how much venom this thing has. And how accurate it is with its spitting. The venom has actually crystallised on my safety glasses. Johann is all smiles for his efforts as he carries the box triumphantly to his office, saying, "I will release it later."

That evening, my last at Mt Nimba, we all sit around in the patio area enjoying our bottles of duty free, every now and then giving a cautionary glance upwards to the tree.

My job done at Mt Nimba, I am back in Conakry on my last day in country; I was on a bit of a sightseeing expedition and looking forward to going home. I notice a police car behind us that has been with us for a bit of time now. A few more turns and yes, this confirmed they are following us, two up. I am following the route I used for the driver training of the Conakry crew a few days earlier so I start to navigate my way back to the office.

"Stevon, mate, we're being followed by the police. I'm heading back to the office. Call Madame Sophia and tell her what is happening please."

I look in the rear-view mirror and now they are flashing their headlights.

"Mr Simon, they want you to pull over."

No worries. Probably just want to check I have a license. So, I pull over at the next opportune spot. Why I don't know, but I tell Stevon and two locals from the Conakry office to keep the windows up and doors locked. Maybe I am just over cautious after having the AK stuck up my nose, but my gut is telling me something is not right. People call it a 'gut feeling' or instinct. It's real and very reliable. It's the part of the human body's natural defence system. What actually happens is that the brain detects danger long before we realise it. As a result, it starts to prepare the body to defend itself with the release of the chemical cocktail and because we have not yet physically responded, the chemicals rushing through the body cause muscle tensioning, increased blood flow to the major organs like the heart and lungs. Blood vacates the stomach, as it's not needed. So that combination results in 'that gut feeling' as we describe it. The most important tip I can give anyone is, listen to it, acknowledge it and most importantly, act on it. Coppers learn this quickly or end up getting hurt. I wind down my window as the policeman approaches.

"Papers."

I hand my international drivers' license to the policeman. He looks at it with disinterest.

"Papers, papers!" he insists.

Okay, that's not the papers he wants. I blankly stare at Stevon and Stevon at me. A light comes on in my head. *Rego papers, he wants the rego papers.* I ask Stevon to get the registration papers for the Landcruiser out of the glove box. He passes them across to me and I pass them in turn to the policeman who shuffles through the couple of pages. He looks at me in disgust and with a little more aggro again he demands, "Papers."

Stevon and I look at each other like, 'what papers is he talking about?' Stevon talks to the policeman.

"Mr Simon, he wants money."

Of course he does. I should have seen that one coming. Well, after being threatened by the spaced-out soldier and now this, I was in no mood to entertain this bullshit and set a precedence for everyone who follows me thereafter.

"No, tell him no, Stevon. I have done nothing wrong."

"Mr Simon, he says if you have no money, you must go to the police station."

Yeah, I bet he does ... trying to put the wind up me. I'll call his bluff.

"Okay, Stevon, tell him we will follow him to the police station."

"Mr Simon, pay him, it's okay and we can go."

I instruct Stevon, "No, we will go to the police station." And with that we follow the police to the local cop shop. "Stay in the car, guys," I tell my passengers.

"Steve." I nod for Stevon to come with me to interpret. Through Stevon's interpreting, I learn the cop now wants the car keys. "No fucking way," is my reply to that.

"We are not allowed to leave the police station," Stevon explains.

Yeah right. Like fuck we're not! I'm thinking.

"We must pay more now," Stevon adds.

Okay, I have had a gutful of this bullshit. I launch into this prick. "I am an Australian here on behalf of the Australian Government at the request of President Conde. You embarrass your president; you insult my government."

Stevon is interpreting this with a look of bewilderment on his face. I pull out my mobile.

"I am calling the Australian Embassy. Steve, mate, tell him I am calling the embassy."

By now we have a bit of an audience gathered. Other police from inside the station have come out to see what was going on; who is this white man at their police station? Who I can only assume is a senior officer or detective appears parting the way between the group that had gathered. He is in a short-sleeved business shirt and trousers, not uniform. There is a conversation between him and the cop who is trying to rip me off.

"Please, pay your fine." His English was not too bad.

"Steve, tell him I am calling the Australian Embassy. Tell him I am here on behalf of the Australian Government. Tell him," I insist.

There is more counsel between Stevon, the uniform cop and the detective and after a few minutes came the reply, "Please sir, it is okay, you may leave."

Holding his hand up as a gesture to stop me calling the embassy, the detective steps off to the side and extends his arm toward the exit.

"Mr Simon, we can go, please." Stevon sounds relieved.

I carry on threatening to call the Australian Embassy and how I am insulted, how the Australian Government has been insulted and this is not the end of it as I climb back into the Landcruiser, gesturing with my mobile. We head for the exit.

"Mr Simon, there is no embassy in Conakry," exclaims Stevon.

"I know there's not, mate. But that prick didn't know."

I smile back and Stevon gives an understanding nod. You might say that maybe I should have given the soldier my camera; maybe I should have given the cop some money. Was my life worth a $150 camera or getting locked up for the sake of a $20 bribe? Of course not. Partly in principle, partly my own stubbornness, but when you're the bunny on the spot, you have a sense for what is going on, what the reality of the situation is. I made the right choice despite what the armchair critics may say otherwise. I am still fuming when we get back to the head office in Conakry. Madame Sophia chuckles as I explain my angst to her and, laughing, she pays it off. "Monsieur, it is the Conakry way."

The next day I fly out heading for KL, Malaysia, having picked up a couple of extra days driver training on the way home. Extra quids, so why not.

My white-knuckle plane ride to Mt Nimba
Shortly after this photo, I had the AK 47 stuck up my nose

The highway in/out of the capital, Conakry

*My 4WD students at base exploration camp Mt Nimba.
The French 'Chef' standing back row, far right.*

Chapter 14

Ring of Fire

You will have heard of the 'Ring of Fire' describing a geographical area of volcanic and seismic activity across Indonesia, including Malaysia to Papua New Guinea. I am about to experience the 'Ring of Fire', doing a four-day weekend in Kuala Lumpur (KL), Malaysia. I had done a day's work of 'Commentary Drives', based on the London Met Police driver training and an excellent method of learning defensive driving and road craft – always good to catch up with the boys again, most of whom I had worked with back in 'The Job'. The accommodation is always first rate when working for this company and, on this trip, we are at the Marriot Hotel, which made up for my misadventures in Guinea. The pay isn't exactly great but then again it isn't hard or dangerous work (I say not 'dangerous' in comparison to other jobs I had done, but then again there had been some 'near death' experiences out on the roads with some of the students). Commentary drives are an excellent method of assessing a driver's hazard perceptions and application of driving methodology. It requires the driver to talk whilst driving, describing what he sees, what he is doing and why. It's an excellent driving system to teach and learn alike and it has not changed a great deal over the many years it has been around.

We're all sitting on couches around the foyer of the Marriot Hotel with our students drinking coffee and doing the assessments. Suddenly, I break out into a cold sweat and the stomach starts cramping up and I'm sure everyone could hear the rumbling and groaning from my gut. Feeling quite uncomfortable, I excuse myself and quickly go to my room. *What is it about lifts when you want to get to your room quickly?* Everyone wants to get on or off at every bloody floor it seems, especially just for me. I am desperate now to get to the toilet before I lose control of my bowels.

Stepping into my room, the sweat is dripping off me, my stomach is doing cartwheels and I am feeling like shit, in the literal sense. Now, I have always thought it is a physical impossibility to vomit and crap all at the same time – oh how wrong I am. No sooner had I sat on the toilet and the arse falls out of my world. Literally. I have never shat so violently as I do now. Sure, I have had the squirts before, expected when living and eating in some of the countries I have. Now, whether it is by good interior design, catering for those suffering with severe gastro in mind, or just coincidence, the bathroom was such so when you are sitting on the dunny you can puke into the hand basin simultaneously as you shit. *Oh thankyou God.* You always hear about people vomiting and the story of carrots in the vomit … not in my case. No carrots for me but some godawful brown mash that resembled nothing that I have ever eaten before. I am puking so hard it feels like I my eyeballs are popping out of my head. All the while my arse is working overtime shooting out the same putrid mash. I think I am going to have to push my bowels back up my arse hole I am shitting that hard. And the smell, it was enough to make you vomit. And I did, again and again and again.

Between flushing the toilet, wiping my arse until it got too sore to wipe anymore, and wiggling my finger around the faucet to wash away whatever had vacated my guts, this is how I remained for the next few hours. I am physically smashed, running a fever; I have ruptured veins in my eyeballs from vomiting so hard. I can barely make it to my bed. I wrap myself up in the sheets and blanket and try to sleep it off, only to be interrupted by the need to make a dash to the toilet and so the whole process starts again. This is how it was for the next twenty-four hours. The sheer volume that I puke and shit out is unbelievable. I know I am dehydrated as I have stopped sweating but still had a fever and my lips are dry, and my mouth feels like the bottom of a cocky's cage. I must be hollow inside by now – it certainly feels like it. I am so weak now I am on my hands and knees going backwards and forwards to the toilet. It gets to the point where I just didn't have the strength to get out of bed, then I farted. Bad move. It just shoots out between the cheeks of my arse and down between my legs. My arse is so red raw I reckon I have been gang raped by the Christian Brothers church choir. There is fuck all I can do but call housekeeping. I pick up the phone located strategically next to the bed, again conveniently located for just occasions, I'm sure. The maid lets herself in and reels back at the stench in the room but somehow manages a smile that is understanding and sympathetic. Skillfully she rolls me to one side and pulls out the sheets from under me, rolling me to the other side doing the same and gathering up the sheet, not spilling a drop of my bodily fluids that had vacated my bowels. Fitting clean sheets, she executes the same moves with skill and finesse. I am going downhill and if I don't do something soon, I will end up in hospital on a drip. *No thank you* and I get on my mobile and call 'Deano', one of the boys I am working with, and ask him to get me some hydrolyte and Imodium. I relay my medical condition to him, but I fail to see the humour in my situation, such is typical of the character of the guys you work with – sympathy is very seldom given. *Toughen up and drink some cement. Fuck you very much.*

I need to get this under control as we are due to fly out tomorrow and no way am I fit to fly. Somewhere along the way I have fallen asleep and, at whatever time it is, there is a knock at the door. I drag myself out of bed and use the wall to hold myself up, I am that weak. I answer the door without turning the room lights on as any light hurts my eyes and I have the headache from hell. I must look like shite. Deano is standing at the door and his face just drops. He seriously didn't think I was this bad until he saw me. So began my regime of hydrolyte drinks, Panadol for the fever and Imodium to close the orifices. As a precaution, I call home to tell the wife I might not be coming home as expected. Whilst concerned, she is used to me not coming home on time, such is the nature of my work. For the next twelve hours, I sleep, I drink, I sleep and I take my medicine and, by the time I am due to fly home, I still feel very delicate indeed. It takes all my effort to get dressed.

The ride to the airport is testing but at least the taxi is air-conditioned, keeping back the stifling heat of KL. The smells of the cafes and restaurants at the airport turn my stomach and I breakout into a cold sweat. *Oh no, I am not going to make it.* I gingerly walk the terminal to the check-in. Hell, my arse is so sore I think it is bleeding, or at least it feels like it.

At check-in, I request an aisle seat near the toilets. Thankfully the Malaysians have stopped scanning for H1N1 (Avian Flu), otherwise men in HAZMAT suits would have been dragging me off to quarantine when they see my heat signature on the screen. The flight home is the longest short haul I have ever done. My guts are making some really strange gurgling noises. Now let me tell you, passengers who have B.O. (Body Odour) should not be allowed to board flights. Apart from being fucking ignorant and rude, and never mind personal hygiene, what about the consideration for the comfort of the other passengers, me, my comfort, thank you very much! This Malay Indian national sitting adjacent to me fucking stinks. Every time he moves a pungent odour of stale sweat attacks my senses and I break into another cold sweat and start to dry retch. It's not possible that I had anything left to puke up and, as if to stick the knife in, the trolley dollies come around with food service and, of course, it is Malaysian cuisine with heavy Indian influences. I swear they are conspiring against me and my delicate disposition today. In preparation, I have one leg out into the aisle just in case I need to make a bolt for the toilets. Thankfully, I make it home without having to leave my seat. The Imodium has done its thing.

Now whenever I travel, I keep a tube of Benpanthen in my wash bag. It's particularly soothing when applied to a red raw rectum. I get home and reassess my business options.

After nine years since leaving 'The Job' (Police Force), I am doing alright but I can do better, there's only so many hours in the day and I am burning the candle at both ends. Something is going to give and it will be either me or the business. I had put too much time and effort in it to see it suffer and I figure, with help, it would take the pressure off me a bit by sharing the workload and I would be able to grow the business. I made the decision to look for a business partner. Now they say never go into business with family or friends. I took heed of that advice.

Chapter 15

Indonesia

In 2009, I merge my business with another entity after nine years of flying solo and, after four years, basically the partnership goes tits up and I walk away in 2013. My former partners are immoral businessmen without conscious and nearly send me bankrupt, with no real plan as to what I am going to do. Then an old mate of mine, GT, from the TRG days, who is now tied up with OAM Group, another successful risk management company run by ex SASR guys, offers me the job of country training manager on a project in Indonesia. He tells me if I am up for it, I will be running a team of guys: Hemi, a former New Zealand SAS soldier, a couple of local terps, an expat Philippino, and about ninety SATPAM Indonesian security personnel. SATPAM is the training and licensing regime that Indonesian nationals undertake to become licensed security guards.

Of course, I jump at the opportunity. Diplomacy was over between me and my former business partners and I needed to earn. I was verging on being bankrupt and losing the family home – so it's off to Indonesia. I will sort the other shit out when I get back in a month or six.

OAM has an apartment in the district of Kuningan, Jakarta, and Hemi and I live here for around five or six weeks preparing the training manuals whilst we wait for our 'KITAS' (work visa) to be approved so we can legitimately work in Indonesia. Finally, the KITAS comes through, but to activate them it is necessary to leave the country, get the KITAS and my passport stamped in and out of Indo by immigration, and then we were right to work. *Singapore, here we come and only a short flight from Jakarta.*

Staying at the Orchard Parade Hotel puts us pretty much slap-bang in the middle of the famous night life of Singapore's 'Lady Boys'. Hemi and I have become good mates. He knows Singapore well, having been stationed here while doing his jungle warfare training. Last time I was in Singapore was as a kid on holidays with my mum and dad, so I knew nothing of the entertainment that was Orchard Road. Hemi tells me about the night clubs and prostitutes so, of course, we just had to go and have a look.

Orchard Towers is fondly known as *Four Floors of Whores*, and with good reason. There is a plethora of girls, lady boys, he/she's loitering on the footpath around the Towers touting for business. The building itself is basically a four-storey brothel lit up in neon lights, with bars and strip clubs pumping out music and a few eateries and shops. As we step onto the footpath out the front, we are offered the company of some very beautiful Asian girls and with some good-spirited banter we go inside and start to explore the four levels of entertainment, eventually deciding on a bar, rather than a strip joint. Everyone is scamming for a dollar every way they can, and this bar seemed to be less mercenary than the rest. The beer is cold, but expensive, and the music is okay.

I have heard about the lady boys and every time one came and spoke to me, I would check out their 'Adam's apple' and hands for those tell-tale man features. Two ladies come and sit at our table, one is dressed in a Wonder Woman outfit and the other is wearing a traditional silk Singaporean dress that accentuated her curves. Their English is very good. We lay the ground rules: we're not here for sex, just to have a cold beer and I think they are both pleasantly surprised at this and we end up having a good laugh with them. We buy them a few drinks, for the pleasure of their company and conversation, of course. Everything comes with a price. As it turns out they are both from Thailand and are hocking their bodies to make money to send home to their families. This is common in Asia where prostitution, although illegal, is generally tolerated. The respective governments will have crack downs on the industry from time to time for the benefit of the international public perception and to keep the organised crime syndicates in check. Many girls prostitute themselves to supplement the poor wages they earn as bank clerks and retail assistants. Sad really, that they feel they have to prostitute themselves, as many are well educated. The drinks are expensive and that's how the establishments make their money, as well as taking a percentage off the girls' earnings.

The two girls want to know everything about Australia and New Zealand. The evening passes quickly and before I know it, it is two a.m. and we have to be at Changi Airport at seven a.m. to get our flight back to Jakarta. We bid the girls farewell and leave them to start up conversation with a couple of old fat bastards with greasy hair tied back in ponytails trying hard to look hip and hoping to get a root because they can't get one back home. *Sad old pricks.*

For the past five months the training team has been travelling throughout the mine sites on East Kalimantan (Indonesian Borneo) and Bogor on the mainland, training the client's security personnel in Riot Control and Body Guarding. The contract is with an Indonesian mining company to train up their internal security force. Hemi and I have a lot in common. Hemi is a fitness freak. He is also ex-police, had been to Iraq and is into his rugby, mainly union but also league. His age, undisclosed, but he can embarrass men half his vintage with his phenomenal build – not huge, just well-proportioned and lean, and abs on him like a Greek God. Hemi is just the tonic I need. At my next assignment in PNG, I am to meet a number of Kiwis who know Hemi and he is well regarded by all. Just goes to show that it is really a small world.

Hemi gets me back in the gym training and I am feeling good for it, dropping the kilos gained from being stuck working behind a desk most days back home. For the first time since I can remember, I get down to 100kg. The man trains like an animal with the ghetto blaster cranked up, screaming out the latest tracks as we smash the weights. At the end of each day, we hit the gym having sweated piss-loads already during the day training the guards. Most of the sites we work at have a gym.

These operations are known in the mining game as "Brownfields" meaning established production. The camps are situated in a clearing of the jungle with an access road circling the camp leading out to the mining site. Originally the camp infrastructure had been established by an Australian mining giant which eventually handed over to the Indonesians. Unfortunately, the locals had not properly maintained the gyms and the equipment was in disrepair, but with the basic dumb bells and bars, it was enough to get a workout done. We start with a warmup, going for a jog around the camp. In 39 degrees and 90% humidity, it doesn't take long to warmup.

On this particular day I am jogging around the camp and Hemi was jogging around in the opposite direction. As I run the access road, I take in the peace of the jungle whilst keeping an eye underfoot so as not to roll an ankle on the loose shale laid to give mine vehicles some traction in the mud when it rains. Unknown to either of us, we are being watched by a third party from the jungle. Why I don't know, maybe it was that 'gut feeling', but for some reason I turn around. Maybe I heard something, I am not alone. Charging out of the jungle at me is this fuck-off big monkey baring its teeth and screeching at me. Later I was to find out it is the Alpha male of a troop of monkeys living in the jungle surrounding the camp. I focus on its teeth – how could I not with two big sharp incisors gnashing at me? Googling later, I find out this particular species of monkey can crush the shells of mud crabs and open coconuts with its teeth. I scream like a bitch. Shock, surprise, fear ... I don't know ... but that's what I do and thankfully it is to my benefit: the monkey stops dead in its tracks. Probably it is as surprised as I am shit scared. *What the fuck am I going to do? I won't be able to outrun it and if it gets hold of me it will rip into me doing some serious damage.* I carry on screaming at it and waving my arms about, trying to make myself look as big and scary as I can – an equal adversary if you like. It works! The monkey looks around quizzically as if to ask, 'Who the fuck is this idiot?' This gives me enough time to take a few more backward steps and pick up some rocks. Hurling the rocks at him, I continue to back away still screaming, then I turn tail and hit overdrive, continuously looking over my shoulder at the Alpha male, still sitting on the road looking puzzled by my antics. *Jesus Christ, I nearly got bitten by a snake in Bogor and now a fucking monkey wants to rip my head off.*

Back in Bogor we had done the initial training in the basics, such as the use of the riot baton, formations and command and control. Bogor is about an hour out of Jakarta, up in the hills where it is a bit cooler, very green and fresh clean air, a pleasant change after breathing the polluted air of Jakarta. But it rains every afternoon. We stay at a privately owned security training complex. It is live-in, quite comfortable, and the food is good.

One day, I have done my laundry and manage to get it dry before the afternoon rains came. When the first drops hit the parade ground in the afternoon, they immediately turn into steam on the hot ground; that's the reminder to go collect my laundry off the line, so I head for the laundry at the back of our quarters. As I step across the storm drain that catches the deluge of rain, something catches my eye and, in mid-step, I look down. Directly below me in the storm drain is this snake, rearing itself up toward me. Like John Cleese doing his Nazi goose step impersonation, I do an about-turn mid-stride and jump clear of the snake. The snake is black and slender and looks poisonous. What does a poisonous snake look like? I don't know – like this fucker! Just within my reach and conveniently next to the laundry is a shovel which I quickly grab and ferociously attack the snake with it. When I am finished, the snake is chopped up into bite-size pieces like a sushi roll. I still manage to get my clothes of the line reasonably dry.

Now, back to my warm-up in the jungle, with the monkey. Hemi and I cross over on our way round the access road and I tell him about my encounter with the monkey and, yep, he just laughs and keeps going, thanking me for the warning. I don't think he really believes me. I keep myself armed with some rocks and as I come back around, I scan the jungle edge. Sure enough, the monkey is sitting just off the road and decides to have another go. I hurl more rocks at him and run backwards, eyeballing him as I put distance between us. Crossing over for the second time, Hemi has fashioned a tree branch into a spear for his protection. The monkey has had a go at him as well. My turn to laugh and say, "I told you so."

For the next three laps it is all eyes on the jungle. Thankfully, the monkey has grown tired of us, realising we are not a challenge to his harem and has retreated back into the jungle. That night at dinner, we are told by the locals that that particular Alpha male had caused all manner of trouble at the camp, attacking vehicles, ripping off windscreen wipers and side mirrors. It had even bailed up one of the miners in his room, banging on his window and trying to get inside. *Must have fancied him!* The locals are reluctant to do anything about it. This particular species of monkey is protected in East Kalimantan and besides, no one is willing to take the bloody creature on. Can't say I blame them either.

Getting around Indonesia can be an 'interesting' experience, if not even death-defying at times. We travel by car, light plane, commercial carriers and small pilot boats. In East Kalimantan, most of the movement between the mine-sites was by light aircraft, a Cessna Caravan that flies relatively low and is operated by a local aviation contractor. Slow and noisy, it is susceptible to the air turbulence over the jungle and we experience every bump, but the scenery is spectacular. At most, flights take only around ninety minutes. But it is a plane with no redundancy, a single engine prop, so the 'safer' option is to travel by road. At least that is the theory. But it means at least six hours driving on the road. You have to weigh up the likelihood and consequences and accept the trade-offs. No redundancy ... or six hours on the road with a suicide jockey. Trust me, flying is safer. Having said that, a couple of years back, sadly an Australian mining company lost the majority of their board as well as a risk advisor on a flight just over the Cameroon border in the DRC when their single engine plane went down in thick jungle.

There are occasions when I had no option but to go by road – once on an unscheduled return to Jakarta, and another when the regular charter flight was fully booked. The mining company hires me a local driver who thinks he is Tommi Makinen, the rally driving champ who only knows one speed and that is flat out. The only time we stop is when I ask to go buy a drink or have a nervous pee, one usually following the other. Fuck me, we hurtle down the roads that in places are no more than the width of the car, overtake on hills and corners, and come close to having several head-on crashes. It is scary. I'm sure a few coats of paint are missing, we come that close to passing vehicles. Hard shoulders are washed away by the constant rain and we traverse the road on two wheels, hitting potholes at full tilt. I hate to think what damage the wheel rims and suspension is suffering. 'Tommi' plays his version of Asian reggae on the stereo, wears fake Ray Ban sunglasses and flashes his pearly whites at me every five minutes in a reassuring grin whilst constantly hitting the horn – why the fuck I don't know, as no one in an oncoming vehicle is going to hear him and everyone he overtakes ignores him. I much prefer that he keeps looking to the front and not me, sitting there terrified on the backseat. Hemi and I chose to sleep on these trips – better we don't see our pending doom if it is to happen.

We arrive in one piece at the capital of East Kalimantan, Banjarmasin, to head to Jakarta. The only commercial service who flies this route is an Indonesian-owned and operated carrier, *Lion Air*, with a poor reputation for safety. It is rumoured that the cabin crew are partial to a bit of 'marching powder' from time to time and the pilots are the ones who *didn't* graduate from flight school. They only fly internally as the carrier is not approved to fly international. You pretty much take whatever you like in the way of luggage on board and jam it in wherever it will fit. *So much for load control and seating allocation. First in best dressed.*

"Nah, mate, my ticket says I have the aisle seat *(I had requested)*, not you. Move!"

You have to be firm to the point of almost being rude, otherwise the locals will wave you away or just totally ignore you, playing the 'No speak English' trick. In practised response, my Bahasa is improving greatly which catches them off-guard and I ask them to move.

"Keluar dari tempat dudukku."

The trolley dollies leave you to it. In fact, I don't know what they do, other than sit up front looking pretty.

The worst passengers are the Hadji group tours on religious pilgrimage. Mostly the groups are made up of the elderly, dressed in crisp white cotton hijabs and sporting the group tour agent travel bag. They will bump and push you out of the way as if in fear of missing out on a seat, even though they have a ticket. It is what it is. In a city of 25 million people, I guess you need to make your way or get pushed to the back of the line, for everything. Landing is worse. Some passengers are up and out of their seat, grabbing their bags from the overhead locker as the plane is making its final landing approach, making phone calls on their mobiles or just moving toward the exit. Everyone in Indonesia has a Blackberry and calls cost about 5 cents, so they go for it 24/7, no matter where or what they are doing. Lion Air had a plane fall short of the runway at Denpasar, Bali, around the same time I holidayed in Bali and I recall seeing the plane still in the water with the tail sticking up out of the water – pilot error, by all account. Thankfully no one was killed. And here we are flying Lion Air.

Their risk management response to the crash was to paint over the Lion Air logo on the tail. But what else can you do when it's the only bloody choice.

Indonesia is a hoot. Hemi has got me fit, the work and pay is good, and we have had some big nights in Jakarta. I love the food and it is always fresh and plenty of it. We patronise one particular bar when in Jakarta, close to the apartment where we stay when in town. BATS, better known as the Bar at The Shangri-La, where the security is reasonable and the music is middle of the road with a mix of a live band and a DJ. Located in a basement of the hotel, the beer is cold and spirits are reasonably priced. I don't think there is any one time that we walked out of there sober, and in the morning, we will sweat it out again in the gym at the apartment before cooking ourselves up a storm for breakfast back in our room.

One particular night at BATS, it is pumping with locals and expats and the band is hammering out a good cover version of the Divinyl's hit I Touch Myself. It is standing room only. We spot a small pedestal table near the corner of the bar and the dance floor, a prime OP, and we make straight for it, only to find it is reserved for 'Larry and Conrad'. I look at my watch, Larry and Conrad are running late. The Reserve note is promptly turned into confetti and sprinkled around the floor of the club and we help ourselves to the platter of complimentary canapés – they will turn stale if we leave them for Larry and Conrad – a hostess giving us a second look as we demolish the platter. We are not Larry and Conrad. Shock, horror, well don't book a fucking table on a busy Friday night and come late expecting it still to be there waiting for you! I am on my third single malt and Hemi on his third JD's. The dance floor is pumping, and the eye candy is pleasing. We have prime position. A waitress places a bottle of Absolut Vodka on the table. I look at Hemi and Hemi looks at me. 'I didn't order a bottle' was the look we gave each other, but hey, thank you kindly, we'll take it anyway.

"No please, mister, this for Mr Laaarry," says the waitress in her best English with a worried smile on her face.

The club reserves bottles of spirits behind the bar for their regulars. Good idea but fuck me, a bottle of Absolut? I can understand it if it's a 25-year-old bottle of single malt Glenmorange Scotch, but vodka, mixed with shitty Coca-Cola? This Larry must be some kind of a wanker. And he is.

The mythical Larry and his sidekick Conrad appear at our table. No sooner do they open their mouths and yep, they are Seppo's and so full of their own self-importance. Don't get me wrong, I worked with some top Americans over in Iraq and I reckon they tend to get a rough deal as the world's police, but they do like everyone to know they are American and, talk loud to make sure. Hemi looks at me, rolls his eyes and tilts his head up, looking at Larry and Conrad and enquires, "S'up Bro?" A classic Kiwi line.

Larry and Conrad stand there like stunned mullets, the looks on their faces saying 'Goddamn, how dare someone else take our table, we're god damn American, don't you know!'

I look at Larry who is now pouting and looks at the hostess like 'what the fuck?' I don't want to see her get into any trouble because of us, so I give the Bro a wink as to indicate 'watch this'.

"Guys, here, put your drinks on our table," as I pass the empty canapé platter to the hostess. "No worries, they can share our table."

She tries to explain that Larry and Conrad have this table reserved and I explain we didn't know, there was no 'Reserved' sign on the table, and we have been here for two hours and no one has said anything to us. She got my drift, smiles, nods knowingly and walks off. Larry and Conrad are obviously ill at ease. We aren't aggressive, not at all, but we hold presence and confidence in our body language. Larry and Conrad look like pasty librarians and stand away from the pedestal table muttering to each other, sipping their vodka mixers, glancing our way and really wanting to put their drinks on 'our' table. We grin, and every time they look at us, we raise our drinks to them.

"Hey bro.," Hemi would say every time.

These blokes are fucked. They don't know where to look or what to do. Gradually, our proxemics pushes Larry and Conrad away. We don't have to say anything, they are intimidated by us, whether they realise it or not. Our personal space is much bigger than the average person's, something you learn to develop as a cop.

One another night, we are accosted by these models, beauty queens or whatever they are, with sashes over their shoulders advertising 1st, 2nd and 3rd places. They are gorgeous and for some reason they all want their photo taken with me and the Bro. I do the standard check to make sure they're not 'lady boy's'. It's great for our egos but apparently more so for the girls. We are about to leave BATS as it is a quiet night in the club, and we have a big day coming up. I reckon these girls would be high maintenance. They are glammed up to the max and you can see they think their shit don't stink and are encouraged to believe it by their minders. I don't know if it is dress jewellery or the real thing, but they have diamonds dripping off their ears and around their necks. The minders are running around after them, fetching this, doing that for them. All we have to do is talk to them and pose with them for photos. I think they enjoy Hemi and me being red hot-blooded heterosexual males, not this metrosexual crap that is apparently the 'in-thing' for men to get in touch with their feminine side. Bullshit! Men are men; they don't have a 'feminine side' otherwise they would be a woman, or gay. I reckon women like this metrosexual thing because the metrosexual is a soft cock and the girls don't have to worry about the guy putting the hard word on them. Hey, I'm all for having a massage and even a traditional shave with a cut-throat, shaving soap and brush and a hot towel bath afterwards, best shave you'll ever have. But manicures and pedicures and getting your eyebrows, back, sack and crack waxed, fuck off! Truth be known, women love men who get dirt under their fingernails, do hard work and are, well you know, men. So often models, movie stars and the like are surrounded by 'metrosexuals', a bit like air cabin crew. If you're aircrew and straight, you could fuck yourself stupid in the 'Mile High Club'. Each to their own, whatever floats your boat.

Anyway, whatever, this evening is certainly doing a whole lot of good for our egos too. The girls are loving it big time, giggling and whispering to one another, leaning over to have selfies with Hemi and me. The drinks are flowing and we're not paying a cent, even better, and this is all out in the foyer of the hotel and we are getting some indifferent looks from hotel staff and patrons alike. Eventually we have to go and we leave the girls walking to their waiting limo, and us to our hailed blue taxi.

Sadly, after six months the contract came to an end. It was Ramadan, and the client in their infinite wisdom has decided that their security element could stand alone, and we are no longer needed. We have done a good job training the teams up and, credit where credit is due, they are holding their own. I guess time will tell and I wish them all the best. A great bunch of blokes.

Hemi has picked up a gig in Kurdistan, northern Iraq doing PSD and I have got a gig in PNG. Our last night in Indonesia is a big one at the BATS. I stagger through the door of our apartment in Kunningan at God knows what time, grab my bag I had packed earlier in prep of a big last stand and stumble into the waiting taxi to catch the 0600hr flight home to Australia. Feeling somewhat seedy, I soak up the alcohol I have consumed in the wee hours with a huge plate of nasi goreng – which has become my staple diet – and a bottle of water in the Garuda business lounge. It goes a long way to sober me up and, feeling somewhat more human, I sleep most of the way home.

Riot Training. Bogor, Indonesia

Baton Training, Bogor, Indonesia

VALE. Hemi Williams

In 2016, I am working for OAM Group on a project in Mali. I learn that I will be once again working with Hemi and I can't be happier. Since Indonesia, he has been working in northern Iraq/Kurdistan and in typical fashion, Hemi has endeared himself to everyone on the Mali project. Before I get in country, Hemi suffers a massive stroke from an undiagnosed condition and is medevac'd out to Paris and eventually home to his beloved NZ and, with his family by his side, he passes away. Hemi Williams, a true gentleman; honoured to call him a friend and to have had the opportunity to have worked alongside such a charismatic man.

Chapter 16

Manus Island

There has been much political and public debate about Prime Minister Tony Abbott's policy on asylum seekers and the establishment of offshore detention centres. I have picked up a gig as a security officer working for global security giant G4S who have been awarded the contract to run the detention centre at Manus Island, Papua New Guinea (PNG). The pollies preferred to call the detention centre a "Processing Centre" and the asylum seekers "Transferees", who are not being detained but processed to be relocated to a participating signatory country (PNG) or repatriated home – it was the choice of the individual. If living in a fenced compound you cannot walk out of on your own free will, with your movements restricted and behaviour monitored 24/7 by security, and required to wear ID cards is not a detention then I don't know what the fuck is. After all, they had tried to enter Australia illegally. You enter illegally via an airport and are caught you are placed in a holding cell (a detention cell) at the airport and returned home on the next available flight.

In this case, they arrive by boat and are caught. They are illegal immigrants. But then they cry asylum which presents a whole new political and legal minefield. Most are from the Middle East and in their mid-20's to early 30s, so most are of military service age, educated and literate. Sure, some had experienced torture, religious or cultural persecution and for these guys I did empathise, but for 99% of them it is a lifestyle change they are seeking; they are 'economic refugees'. In fact, I met an Iraqi that had been a police recruit trained at the military base where I had the contract as a Training Advisor during Operation Iraqi Freedom in 2005. They are not refugees or asylum seekers; they had left families behind, by choice. They spent thousands of dollars to travel around the world chancing their luck by jumping on a fishing boat operated by people smugglers (organised crime) expecting to be taken to Australia. The immigration system has been exploited for a number of years and how they were entering Australia was illegal.

It is common knowledge that Australia is viewed as a soft touch. That was until the fall out between Julia Gillard and Kevin Rudd saw a change in our country's leadership and political will. Despite all the media coverage and efforts of the new Liberal government to publicise internationally the change in policy, these people still believe they have a right to come to Australia – a right, not a privilege – *their* right. Go figure. What would happen if I try to enter their country illegally, I'm pretty sure we can all guess the answer to that!

For most part, I find the 'Transferees' arrogant, rude, liars and insightful. They expect everything to be handed to them on a plate, and it pretty much is.

"I pay to go Australia. I not want come here. I want to go Australia."

My reply was standard, I am not about to give these people any false illusions. "No you won't. You can either stay in PNG or be sent back home."

"But I want to go to Australia!"

And my reply again is standard. "What you have done is illegal."

To them, they could not see anything wrong with what they have done.

"Why did you not apply to immigrate to Australia like other

people do and you could bring your family?" I ask.

The response is one of indignance and defiance, "I not want to wait. I like Australia. Australia very good. I want to live in Australia."

Time and time again I hear this as their justification.

On arrival at the detention centre, many of the illegal immigrants have t-shirts from Bali and Phuket, mobile phones, Ray-Ban sunglasses, designer jeans and croc sandals in their personal belongings.

"I have holiday before I leave to go Australia," is a fond and common explanation. But what the public get to see on TV is these poor refugees with just the shorts, thongs and a t-shirt they are wearing, poor souls. Let's understand one thing here: they chose to do this; they chose to get on a leaky boat with limited food and water. Why? As a way of strengthening their claim as an asylum seeker, to con the Australian government and the Australian people. To gain sympathy. One particular lad is quite open about his flaunting of the immigration system.

"If I get sent home, your government give me $3,000. No problem. I have girlfriend in London, maybe I go see her. I have done before. Maybe next time I get to Australia."

Many are of the mistaken belief that if they destroy their credentials that will somehow support their claim to be a 'refugee' and expedite their passage to Australia. In fact, it was the opposite. But again, somehow, they perceive this as Australia's fault that it took so long to verify their identity and country of origin. Not deterred by the first unsuccessful attempt they are prepared to do it again, and do it again, illegally.

Because of the lack of bona fide identification, vetting is difficult, particularly with the countries they come from that have less than efficient social services and security records. Did they have a criminal record or were they wanted for a crime committed in their own country or somewhere in between on their global trek?

I witness the same activity in the detention centre that goes on in any mainstream prison. Standover and intimidation, distillation of alcohol, making of weapons, stealing and assault. This is not something that a law-abiding member of the community just simply turns their hand to. I am certain many were criminals and possibly sympathetic to a terrorist insurgency group. Each compound has their own gangs ruling the general population and running their rackets, segregating themselves according to nationality and religion. There is no way they are going to integrate into Australian society. This is the risk if temporary protection visas into Australia are issued. There are presently some thirty-five thousand asylum seekers on temporary protection visas already living in Australia. Perhaps that was the real purpose of not having a passport or Gencia.

Global terrorism is very real and there can be no certainty of who these people are who are trying to enter Australia, or why. Are these the kind of new Australians we wanted? No, Mr Abbott has got it right.

(At the time of writing this chapter, ISIS or IS were rampaging through Iraq and Syria beheading non- believers, and Britain had raised their terror alert to "severe" due to the home-grown terror threat in their country. Australia was contending with its own problems with foreign nationals leaving to go and fight in the Jihad – these same people had sought refuge and protection in the west some years before under the previous Government policy).

Don't get me wrong, I discriminate equally. I have no problem with the government issuing 4500 protection visas to the Yazidi fleeing the persecution and genocide of ISIS in the north of Iraq and having to take refuge on Mt Sinjar to escape. These, and others who have suffered similar fates in other countries, are the real refugees.

The illegal immigrants are given free packets of cigarettes, soft drink, chocolate, internet access and a phone card as a reward for attending an English language lesson or some other personal development class, or for some other BS reason, for being a good boy would do. Soft drinks and lollies I can accept but cigarettes and free internet and telephone, no. Who were they calling? What websites are they accessing on the internet? We cannot monitor their calls or look over their shoulder when they are on the internet – that would be a breach of their civil liberties. I can see it now in the headlines: 'Refugee with lung cancer sues Australian Government'. There are shipping containers full of cartons of Pall Mall cigarettes just for the illegals, along with pallets of other assorted goodies, all for them. How did they thank the Australian government? … by vandalising brand new amenities and ablution blocks installed for their sole use. They shit all over the toilets, shove empty water bottles and rolls of toilet paper down the toilet bowl, bunging up the plumbing. The doors and control knobs are broken, wrenched off the washing machines, just wanton vandalism. Why? Because they know it fucks everyone about and they get mileage out of it through the media.

'Look at the conditions we have to endure. Look how we are being treated'.

Mealtimes are just chaos. They treat the mess halls as 24/7 restaurants, coming and going as they pleased expecting to be fed anytime, despite mealtimes clearly posted on the mess halls. Every day they bang on the doors demanding entry, despite the dining hall and kitchens being in darkness. 'Mister, I sleep. You no wake me. I want to eat now.'

Oh, I'm so sorry. Let me go wake up the chef and see if he can whip something up for you. *Yeah right!* No one could or wanted to wait their turn in an orderly fashion of something that resembled such. Anti-authoritarian and anti-establishment is the order of the day. Many eat like pigs (no pun intended), I have never seen people eat like this anywhere, and I have been to a lot of places. No one eats like this, except at the Manus Island RPC it would appear. Beggars belief. I am staggered at the amount of food wasted by them. They get a choice of hot and cold selection at every meal; water, tea, coffee, juice and fruit – fruit which they try and smuggle back to their dormitory to brew alcohol. It explains why two to three bags of sugar disappear each morning and afternoon from the tea and coffee making stations in each of the compounds. They fill their plate to overflowing with food only to throw half of it away in the rubbish bin. Whole steaks and they take two just because they can and then throw them in the rubbish bin, wasted. But they still complain.

"Mister, this food, it is shit."

Now where have I heard that before as they shove their plate at you?

I am told there is no portion sizing by the caterers, as per a directive from DIAC (Department of Immigration and Citizenship) apparently. These people are just taking the piss because they know that the soft cock political minorities and 'do-gooders' will scream loudly if they complain to them about their 'treatment'. But no, I don't see the bleeding-heart humanitarians and welfare groups jumping up and down about the local Manus Island native villagers going without the basic necessities of life such as clean running water and all the other essential utilities. Who is really suffering the injustice, I wonder.

It would seem that human rights discriminates also. As for some of the stakeholders operating in the detention centre, I shake my head in disbelief. The welfare agency engaged employs young and impressionable perky girls in their twenties with the misguided fantasy that their spiritual contribution is going to change the world. They enter the compounds, wearing cut off denim shorts and polo shirts tied in a knot at the front, showing off their midriff and wander into the compounds by themselves with groups of virile men, and go inside the accommodation blocks, by themselves, absolutely clueless.

I try and express my concerns for their safety, and I just cannot get the message across to them. They think I am, along with the rest of security, a heathen. These guys are fucking each other for God's sake. Hello, is this not a red flag to the girls. They have seen the rape victims being assisted to the medical centre for treatment.

(I personally did not see or hear of any physical or sexual abuse towards the detainees by either local or expat security guards. Sure, there were the dickheads like you get in any job and some were sacked. The only assaults taking place were those by the detainees on other detainees, usually Middle Eastern on a weaker minority like the Rohingya).

Maybe it will take one of the girls getting split from ear to arsehole before they understand why we want them to carry their personal duress alarm or be accompanied by a security guard. We know there are razor blades, other weapons and illegal alcohol hidden in the accommodation blocks. We are not allowed to conduct searches unless there is an emergency incident. It is a breach of their civil liberties or some other bullshit. I do lots of 'welfare checks' and if the powers-that-be don't like it, stiff shit.

Then there are the interpreter services. They are never around during the day when you need them and forget it if you want one after hours. As most of them are Muslim, they impose their religious beliefs upon the catering company – no pork products will be served because of their faith. I respect other people's beliefs, religion and culture as you do when in their country, but it also works the other way. In PNG, pork has cultural and social significance and symbolises wealth in their community and is used to trade goods, and forms part of their diet. What about respecting the host countries culture and traditions? I don't know about you, but I enjoy my bacon and eggs on a Sunday morning.

They are not so successful when they try the same stunt in the galley of *HMAS Choules* anchored in the bay. *The Choules* has been brought in to provide additional accommodation for RPC personnel and most of the interpreters and government staff have been billeted on board. The captain gives a definite NO, but in not so diplomatic terms. Now, because the accommodation on *Choules* is five-star in comparison to 'The Swamp', the terps are not about to shit in their own nest, but happy do so in everyone else's. But it gets better: the illegals are provided gym equipment – Olympic standard bars and weights, benches, boxing bags and gloves. There are some pretty big boys amongst them and very handy with their feet and hands, let alone the potential weapons lying around for them to use. They'll fit in well with the Middle Eastern criminal underbelly already well established in Australia. How ludicrous! We don't have a gym (there is a gym on *HMAS Choules*, but the barge only makes two runs a day which conflicts with our shift timings), so guys bring their own gear with them from Australia, like TRX and power bands, light weight and not bulky as we are limited on baggage weight flying to the island. Guys improvise making weights by filling up jerry cans with sand and other designs of ingenuity like affixing the straining post of a fence between the dongers (sleeping quarters converted from shipping containers) as an improvised chin up bar.

To top that off, we are living in converted 20ft shipping containers, sleeping four to six in bunk beds and you can't swing a cat inside – real cosy, and do I mean cosy. And if you had someone whose hygiene is not the best, the donga stinks of farts, sweaty socks and BO.

One accommodation block has the nickname 'The Swamp' as it continuously floods when it rains, which is nearly every day, and you step out into ankle deep mud and water. The walk boards turn into floating rafts you surf to dry land. No TV, no internet or mobile phone reception. That is all up at the detention centre for the refugees, so to phone home you walk halfway to the detention centre before you get any mobile reception. The dongas are not even earthed or fitted with smoke detectors and, with only a couple of power points, everyone is piggy backing their adaptors on top of one another. From an OH&S aspect we are living in breach of so many OH&S regs. But we get on with the job and make the best of a worst situation. I would gladly take a bed in the accommodation blocks inhabited by the detainees, open, spacious, ice-cold air-conditioning.

Gastro is another problem and is rife throughout the camp with hygiene difficult to maintain, given that there are only twenty-odd toilets and showers, all shared between hundreds of security staff 24/7. Getting our laundry done is another bun fight. A few of us take our washing over to the local ladies working at the naval base and pay them to do it for us. It's the little things in life that can make life a little more bearable.

There are quality personnel working here at the detention centre. Former cops and soldiers who have worked in Iraq, Afghanistan, trained and experienced who have done the hard yards, but they are perceived as threats to the incumbent management and are admonished to be security guards forever more. If it is not for the troops on the ground, this whole place would fall apart (it has only lasted as long as it has because of the guys on the ground). Staff turnover is huge, the frustration at the stupidity of management too much for many and they did not return after their first rotation – some left even sooner. One day on the island I think is the record. (I did two rotations and thankfully was head hunted by a risk management company back in Australia before going back for the third).

From Jackson International Airport, we catch a local carrier to Manus Island then bus to the detention centre. The local airline is operated much to the same standards I had observed in Africa and Indonesia. Thankfully, the national carrier from Australia to PNG is serviced by Qantas. We stay overnight at the five-star Airways Hotel, located next to the airport. A surreptitious way of softening us up before the shit living conditions that are awaiting us at the detention centre.

We hop on the local carrier and the plane just levels off after leaving Jackson's, when suddenly it drops altitude, starts to turn and the pilot begins dumping fuel. We all notice the engines labouring and revs fluctuating, which is a little discerning only forty minutes into the flight as we head back to the mainland. There is a problem with the fuel, so we hang around the departure lounge waiting and hoping to be told we will get to spend another night at the Airways. *You beauty!* But just our luck ... the problem is resolved after a few hours of sitting around in the domestic departure lounge, and we head out north over the blue ocean once more, on the same plane.

No sooner had we levelled off, and I am sure everyone is feeling a little apprehensive, a flight engineer appears and as he looks out through a porthole at the engine on the starboard side, he looks at the guy seated at the window next to it and make a rather nonchalant comment. 'If you see fire in that engine, let me know.'

That's just fucking great. We all laugh it off but are not really amused at the blasé attitude towards safety shown by the local operator of the airline. It was another nail in the coffin of this contract for many of the guys, and a few girls, on board the flight.

The first day back after my ten-day break and start of my second rotation, I am sat in the staff dining area at the detention centre and have just fired up my laptop (the only place you can get Wi-fi) when the shit hits the fan, all at the doing of the illustrious management. There was a blue (a fight) between PNG forces (police and navy) outside the detention centre – nothing to do with the incumbent security or the government stakeholders running the detention centre. But some idiot decides to involve themself in what was going on and gets a 'fuck you too' for sticking their nose in where it don't belong, and hits the panic button. Technically, we have no jurisdiction outside the wire so why the fuck get involved in someone else's problem?

Some silly bastards were running around like headless chooks screaming their box off, telling everyone, "Move to the back of the compound," getting right up into everyone's faces, bright red face and veins popping out on their forehead. It was embarrassing.

"Move to the back of the compound, now," she screams.

Turns out one officer losing their shit on everyone is a former WA Police Officer. More embarrassment.

What the fuck is going on? No one knew at this point. Then, of course, the rumour mill starts to work overtime as it tends to do when people get told fuck all. At one stage, we hear guns have been pointed at staff and the local forces involved are threatening to shoot each other. If there are weapons sighted, what the fuck was some numpty rostering clerk doing getting themselves mixed up in it in the first place? Anyone and everyone were being ushered to the far side of the compound.

I pack up my laptop and do as I am told. Everyone is corralled at the back of the compound with absolutely no clue as to what is going on. For half hour or so we're all huddled up in a disused section of the centre like goldfish in a bowl. Then a second major blunder. The order to evacuate is given, expats only. Expats only. Fuck the local guards and staff with whom we work and have earnt one another's respect. If it's that serious, everyone evacuates.

What is happening is bullshit. Some government official at the centre has stuck their nose into a matter they know fuck all about, and contract management is too spineless to stand up to them as the security provider for fear of getting a non-compliance, that is, having a 'breach of the contract' dropped on them.

The order to evacuate to the emergency assembly area requires us to pass the illegals' compounds. Well, the look on their faces says it all, 'What about us?'

No sooner had we reached the evac point, the word comes down to turn around and come back, and we do 'The Walk of Shame' past the illegals again. We have come a long way to winning the hearts and minds of the illegals, not because we empathise with them but because it is the smart thing to do. It's a fine balance between providing security and maintaining rule of law. We are outnumbered easily, and poorly resourced, and should they, the illegals, ever decide to turn on us we will be well and truly in the shit. The question is already being asked from both sides, the locals and the illegals, 'What was going to happen to us?'

Now, in my book, you look after your own first, no matter what nationality, expat or local national. Do that and you can do your job, which is maintaining the security of the illegals and their evacuation, if it were to become necessary. Neither could be achieved today.

The centre returns to some normality and we learn the real story I have just reverted. The dissemination of misinformation from management in explanation thereafter was laughable and they are in damage control big time, carefully distance themselves from any responsibility and point the finger elsewhere. In time, history would show that they learnt nothing from this incident and subsequent rioting resulted in the death in custody of an illegal and the loss of a multi-million-dollar contract.

I was no longer working at Manus Island when the first riot occurred; I had been headhunted by a risk management company back home. But when I heard about the death of Iranian detainee, Reza Barati, during the riot, I was not surprised. I do not condone the actions of those responsible, but let me be straight about this, the young innocent face portrayed in the media was much different to the Reza Barati I had dealt with at Manus Island.

When he first arrived at the RPC he was suffering from a broken jaw. Barati was an accomplished boxer from Iran, tall and well built. Because of his injury, he was on soft foods and it took quite some time for him to eat. Because of this, he was allowed to jump the queue at mealtimes to allow him extra time to eat. The problem was he then expected to be allowed to jump the queue after he had recovered and was back on solids and, because of his infamy as a boxer, he would use this to intimidate and bully the other detainees in line to let him go to the front. When any of the local PNG guards would try and tell him to take his place and wait in line he would do the same with them. His behaviour also extended into the compound yard, and I often saw him walking around with two or three minions who would make sure Barati got his preferred seat in the dining hall, interrupt another detainee's internet session in the media room, or tell a detainee to get off a piece of gym equipment to allow for Barati's sole use, fetch him a drink, do this or do that. And again, when told he cannot do this and to wait his turn, he would threaten and intimidate the PNG guards.

For me, I was not about to take his shit, but I was not about to have a stand up with him either. There is always another way to skin a cat and he got the message soon enough from me and towed the line when I said so.

It was to be a bad move on Barati's behalf with the local PNG guards. They have a very strong cultural system called *Wontok*, meaning one talk, all one people. Wontok is also a rule by which all locals live. It's very much like our mateship in Australia. Look out for your mates when they need help or are in trouble. But also, mateship is about telling a mate when to pull his head in or give them a reminder to mind their manners. It's a strong bond that is formed. The Wontok system goes further in that it is also used to discipline and punish wrong doers. Depending upon the nature and seriousness of the transgression, Wontok maybe the order of compensation to be paid to the aggrieved, a pig as payment, for instance. Or if serious, tribal punishment, even death. Wontok must be made and they do not forget a debt and it must be honoured or the offending party will receive ongoing payback (punishment). This is why tribes have been warring for years with one another up in the highlands, because of Wontok that happened generations back.

When the riot happened, the PNG guards saw it as an opportunity to exercise Wontok upon Barati, and he suffered the consequences of his own actions. He is beaten to death by the local guards. As you can imagine, this just played beautifully into the hands of the Labor party, civil libertarians and media. Splashed all over the front pages of major news outlets was a picture of the much younger Barati, looking every part of the innocent teenager. This case is still dragged up from time to time when the question of 'boat people', asylum seekers and detention centres arises, which coincidently is usually around every federal election.

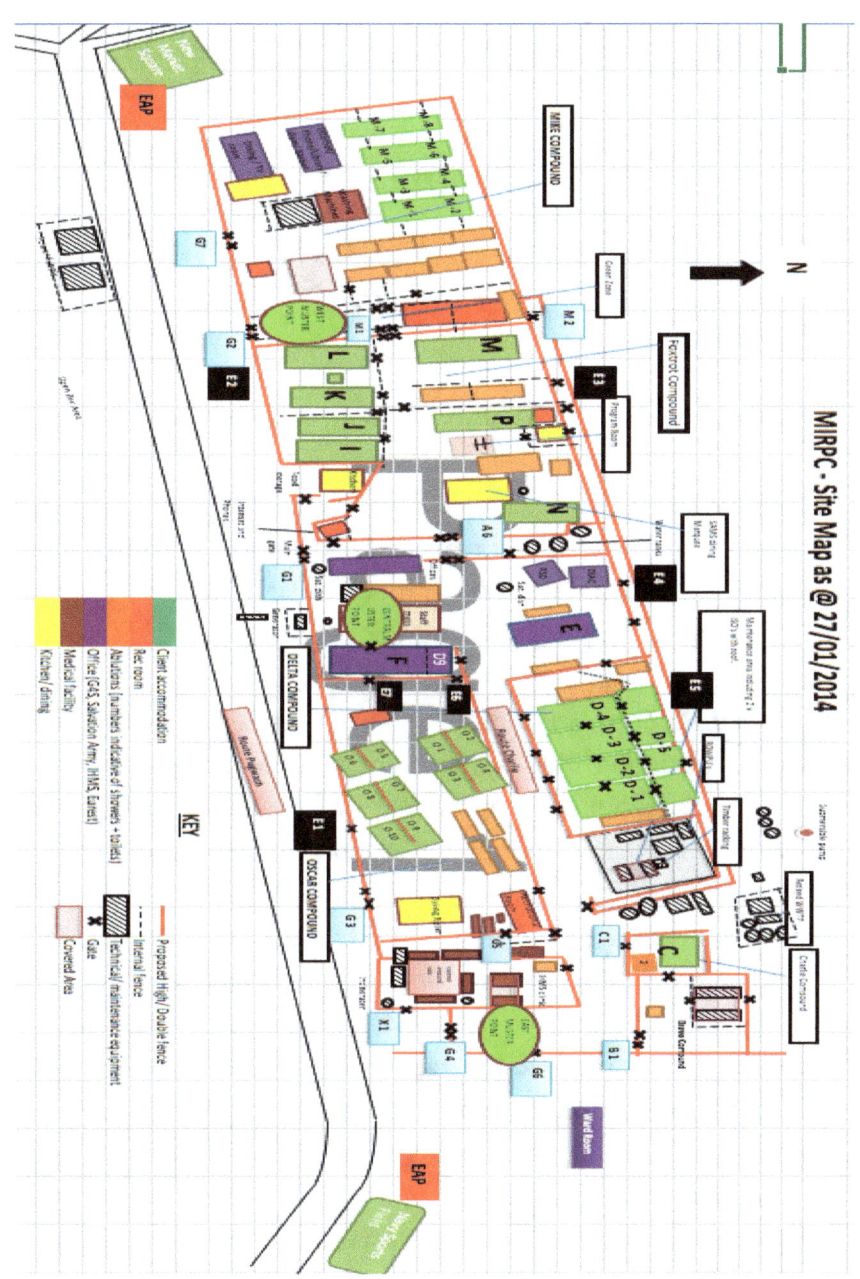

Manus Island Regional Processing Centre

Chapter 17

Tanzania

So back to the ore cart down the mine shaft in Tanzania where we started.

No problem, easy fixed, 'just climb out', I hear you suggest. But here's my dilemma. Question, have the locals forgotten to fuel up the 'gennies' that run the mill, as they regularly do, *useless pricks* or is it the Jarpy's (pronounced 'Yarpee') playing games with the new Aussie boy – *ha ha, very funny, not* – or, ever suspicious (a legacy from being a cop), are the *Askari* setting me up because I have disturbed their nice little arrangement with the Jangali?

All that is stopping me hurtling to my certain death and ending up a pulverised mush slopping around in the ore cart at the bottom of the shaft is a steel cable running up to the millhouse, operated by the Askari. The air is pretty thin in the shaft and very humid and it is getting uncomfortable for this little Vegemite.

Why not call up on the radio and see what the problem is?

Yeah, good one, but the radios we have been given don't transmit this far underground and basically operate in line-of-sight.

I could roll out over the side of the cart and three things could happen. One – nothing, all good. Two, the power could start up again at any moment in which case I could be crushed between the cart and the shaft wall. Or three, the Askari releases the brake cable and I get decapitated. I take the former option and walk out.

So how the fuck did I end up in this situation?

A mate of mine, Tex, a former SASR soldier who was doing very nicely for himself in the world of PSC's (Private Security Contracting) running his company, asked me if I could fill in for him on a contract he had secured in Tanzania. Sure, why not? Good money, $500 a day, all expenses paid, somewhere I hadn't been before, work I haven't done before, a new challenge and a tick on the résumé. *Couldn't be any worse than Guinea or Iraq, surely?*

I'm not ex-SAS or Special Forces, not even ex-military. I'm an ex-cop with a tactical policing background. That's how we met. It's a pretty strong relationship between like-minded men drinking piss together at the RSL on ANZAC Day. The TRG had a good relationship with the SASR being that their base is located in the beachside suburb of Swanbourne in Western Australia and we had been honoured to train with them over the years, hence the relationships. At this point in time, I had been out of 'the job' for some eleven years, during which I'd had a variety of gigs around the world, but I still enjoyed a good relationship with former colleagues and kin.

Tanzania. I had heard of it, somewhere in Africa but where exactly, who knows? I look up good old Wikipedia and find that Tanzania is on the east coast of Africa bordered by Kenya and Uganda to the north, Rwanda/Burundi and DRC to the west and Mozambique to the south. Dar Es Salaam is still considered the capital. I am going to be at an underground mine-site, a three-hour drive south east of Arusha, the closest town of any significance which has Kilimanjaro Airport as its busy gateway.

Like almost all African states, it is rife with corruption, poverty and AIDS. If it's not the locals holding their hand out, it is the police – money, water, food, whatever they can get. You can't help but feel they have been dealt a rough hand. That is not to say that the Bantu tribes of the land aren't still a proud race; but even there you can see western influence slowly decaying their traditional ways. Animal skins and mud make way for plastic tarps and chaff bags covering the wood frames of their huts.

Tanzania is the only place in the world where you can find the blue Tanzanite stone. Other than for jewellery, there isn't much use for it. I arrive in Tanzania, jet-lagged to the max after flying from Australia, plane hopping from 'Jo'burg' to Dar Es Salaam to Arusha and a three-hour drive along corrugated dirt roads, to be greeted by Tex with a wide grin and handing me a cold 'Kili' (Kilimanjaro Beer). The look on his face says it all: 'You've got your work cut out for you, mate'. Quick intros all-round and he's gone – off to secure work elsewhere, such is the nature of PSC's.

I meet Henny, a security supervisor, an expat South African, good fella and his offsider Colin, also security and expat and also a likeable fella. I was to learn that Colin had actually been imprisoned for three months in Arusha for shooting dead a Jangali who was trying to steal ore from the back of a dump truck which Colin was guarding. The Jangali climbed onto the ore truck and attacked Colin with a machete. I got the idea that there had been an exchange of money which had secured his release and understandably his attitude towards the locals was, let's just say, 'testy' at times.

I listen intently to the Jarpy's trying to work my way through their thick accents, with intermittent local Swahili and them frequently breaking into their native Afrikaans. Finally, we reach the mine-site, and I am taken up for a meal at the expat kitchen. With that, I got my head down and crashed until morning.

My brief is to train up the Askari, who are supervised by a contingent of Gurkhas, and to implement operational procedures, make improvements where necessary and generally raise the standard of security operations at the mine. The incumbent security manager is from Zimbabwe and an ex-British Royal Marine called Chris, a man in his early 30s. We become good mates and still talk from time to time today. Chris couldn't be a master of any particular trade as he is doing a plethora of jobs that should be done by the Askari and mine management and in time, I was to find out why. Rudy is another expat who helps Chris out from time to time, but his expertise is IT, and my arrival allows for him to return to his core role.

After breakfast up in the expat kitchen, I go on the grand tour of the mine site. The mine operates 24/7. There are four main shafts, of which two are closed – a typical mine operation like you may find anywhere in Australia, except for one difference. Ringing the lease is the local villages and the illegal operators, and herein lays one of many problems. The labour force and the Askari all come from the local villages, and from the same families. Not hard to see the problem here. And then there are the Jangali who also live in the same villages. Whilst some work for legitimate mining companies, those more enterprising, dig down and across into our mine lease. Some are so bold as to just walk in and enter the closed shafts. My brief has immediately changed. Training is not possible. All available and capable security personnel are working 24/7 underground protecting the shafts.

How the Jangali went about their pillaging was nothing short of staggering. Boys – not men, not teenagers – boys burrow into the dirt like meerkats using a hammer and chisel, lying on their stomachs, slowly chipping away and dragging themselves along as the tunnel gets deeper. At the point daylight no longer reaches them, they strap a torch to their head with rubber strips cut from an old bike inner tube. They keep digging and sorting through the dirt, bagging the Tanzanite as they go. Sometimes they stay underground for up to a week, sustained on some sort of native herbal remedy that would keep them going, and wearing a cloth over the mouth to keep the dust out of the lungs. When they return to the surface, if they returned to the surface, the legal miner would pay them off in food. Hardly a fair exchange. What a desperate fucking existence!

It is not known how many had been crushed to death or

suffocated by cave-ins, but it was certain there were bodies down there, entombed forever. The squashed remains of some had been found by miners and returned to the surface. This is just the way it is.

The larger illicit operations present the bigger problem. Their activity compromised the integrity of the legal mining operations and safety of the miners, with unmapped shafts and tunnels running every which way, like rabbit warrens, all over the lease. At times you can hear the Jangali through the shaft walls digging parallel shafts. When they stop digging is the time to worry because that means they were about to blast. Too much, and not only their shaft but our own could collapse. *Fucking great.*

Compared with western standards, the safety and the structural integrity of the mine shafts are a joke. Even I could see that, and I know jack shit about underground mining. No escape shafts, no emergency rooms, no BA (Breathing Apparatus) – just the main shaft in and out and the working shafts running off – no redundancy systems, meaning no backup whatsoever.

In due course, we discovered the Askari are in cahoots with the Jangali who tell them which shafts are producing Tanzanite, and when the shaft is empty of expats. They get so brazen that the Jangali break through into the working shafts from their opposing shaft and meet with the Askari to discuss 'business'. Don't get me wrong, not all the Askari were dodgy, just most of them.

There is much work to do. Chris and I need to get around the mine site and we procure a couple of 250cc trail bikes. After some basic repairs we get them running and use them to do our patrols around the mine-site.

The villagers steal anything they can sell. The perimeter fence has been broken up and sold off as scrap metal. Plant and machinery are slowly being stripped where it stands, and this is happening all over the mine-site. One morning we ride our motorbikes to the main gate to do an inspection and, situated not more than 100 metres from the gate house is a water tank on a 12-metre-high wooden frame tower – or at least it was yesterday. Someone has come along during the night and stolen it. On questioning the Askari, no one saw or heard anything. Whoever took the water tank would have had to somehow push it off the tower and roll it onto the back of a ute or flatbed truck.

"You must have been asleep?" I questioned.

"No Bwana, not me Bwana, I no sleep."

I guess it is an indication of how poor these people are. Yet incredibly, everyone has a mobile phone, and herein lies yet another problem. Over the days and weeks, I make some interesting discoveries. During our rides around the mine-site, we discover an OP (Observation Post) on the side of a hill overlooking the mine lease. An LUP (Lay Up Point) for the Jangali, but also to conduct obs and provide intel not only to the Jangali but also to the Askari and miners on the movement of Expats. Chris logged the OP on his Garmin.

It is common knowledge that Tanzanite is literally walking out of the mine. Once a shift is over and the miners are topside, they are on their mobiles arranging to meet their illegal brokers. There are tracks running everywhere, crossing over the non-existent fence-line into the villages where the deals are done. That is one way. Even bolder, the brokers, mostly Indian nationals from the jewellery houses in Arusha, wait outside the gatehouse in their BMWs and do their wheeling and dealing right in front of us. But outside the 'wire' we can't touch them.

So how is it done? I mentioned 'literally walking out' ... here's how.

While underground the miner wraps a piece of Tanzanite up in plastic and shoves it up his backside. Topside he disappears into the bushes, retrieves the stone, discards the plastic and simply walks out, all under the observation of an accomplice sitting in the OP on the hillside. There are discarded pieces of plastic wrap laying around everywhere, *nice*. The Askari manning the gatehouse just wave the miners on through, no random searches of course.

About ten days in, it is time to go underground for a look how the Tanzanite is being smuggled to the top. On the surface, security is a basket case but do-able so I am pretty sure it will also be a basket case underground.

I am issued the traditional miner's helmet with lamp and power pack and a pair of rubber wellington safety boots, if you can call them that. Everything comes from China, because it's cheap. The soles of the boots are so thin I might just as well wear thongs. These are general issue at the mine. I ditch them for my own boots that had served me well so far. With a couple of the Jarpy mine engineers, Colin and a Gurkha team leader by the name of Lal, we climb into an ore cart at the number 4 shaft mill house. Thumbs up all round as we start our descent into the dark.

Lal advises me, "Keep your head down, Block."

So here are four of us, squashed up in the ore cart, knees to chins. The top of my helmet just clears the shaft's wooden support beams. Everything is covered in a coarse black dust, a byproduct of mining the Tanzanian earth, and it's not too long before I start to look like Al Jolson. In lurches and jerks, we eventually reach the bottom of the main shaft and clamber out of the cart. I look back up the shaft and can only see darkness.

My eyes adjust to the artificial light as I am led through a maze of tunnels. Overhead, the mono rope runs – a pulley system carrying ore bags filled with dirt – from the mine-face to a hopper, where the ore is dumped through a grill to sort the larger rocks into the ore cart we just rode down in, and taken back to the surface. A couple of Gurkhas stand guard over the hopper, another top side on the conveyor belt that runs up to the crusher. I notice steel bars welded and fixed together, across holes in the shaft walls, as makeshift security grills. This is the attempt to stop the Jangali from entering our shafts from their illegal shafts.

Ducking ore bags constantly moving overhead on the mono rope, we clamber our way through the tunnels, passing the Askari spread out through the tunnel until we arrive at the mine's working face. Colin is to supervise the dig; an Askari oversees the filling of the ore bags, a Gurkha supervises the Askari and the tying of ore bags onto the mono rope, and miners constantly moving back and forth through the tunnel system disappear and reappear. I make a mental note to self about the deployment and placing of security personnel. It's a hive of activity. I sit down in a corner of the working mine-face to get good obs on and keep out of their way.

The mine-face is lit up by a couple of port-a-floods (you know the type you can buy at Bunnings); the air is coming from a compressor which pumps it down from the surface through a ducting system – it has a very metallic taste about it. The miners are slogging away with picks and shovels, breaking up the rock blasted earlier from the face, and filling ore bags for the mono rope. It really isn't too hard to see how they smuggle Tanzanite out. I am watching the goings on when I see a miner place his foot on top of some ore. He is just waiting for an opportunity to pick it up and slip it down the inside of his welly boot.

"Hey, fella," I shout and point to the miner. "Lift your foot up."

Sheepishly, he lifts his foot and Lal grabs the Tanzanite. The evil looks I get from the miners and the Askari says it all. Lal gives me a knowing smile. *That's right fellas, I'm watching you thieving bastards*, I think. Much easier is the pillaging of ore bags along the unguarded sections of mono rope. Empty ore bags litter the floor along the tunnels. When there is a change of shift or tasks, the miners simply step off to one side, pop down an old shaft or into a dark corner – and there are plenty of them – wrap up the stone in plastic to smooth its path, drop their pants and up it goes.

Next thing I know a rumbling noise like a freight train hurtling towards us out of the black tunnel followed by a lot of shouting from further up the tunnel warns us of a rock fall. Instantly the miners press themselves to the walls of the shaft and I immediately adopt the same position. Two big boulders come crashing down, bouncing off the steps terraced into the shaft floor, breaking up into smaller rocks and ricocheting in every direction. No one is hurt, thankfully. Colin explains this happens when a combination of the earth being disturbed by the digging and exposure to the air pumped into the shaft leaves huge slabs hanging on the ceilings of the tunnels and walls. In time, it simply falls away. He points to a huge slab still hanging overhead from the roof of the tunnel, hanging for now, anyway. I think back to the Jangali boys crushed in their little tunnels, never to be recovered. I think Colin can tell what I am thinking about; and tells me, "This sort of mining operation wouldn't be allowed at home."

No shit, I think. I make another mental note about the procedures at the mine-face. Fresh eyes offer an opportunity to see things differently. The Jarpy's and the Gurkhas are doing the best they can, given the resources, but things have to change. I will discuss strategies with the management later. Then all of a sudden, without warning, we are plunged into pitch black darkness and almost total silence. *Fuck*! My mind is going a hundred mile an hour. *This just keeps getting better. What now!* Then a yellow light appears, like the morning star just above the horizon, then another and another and another. The miner's helmet lights are being turned on. Then torches come on as well. Dull yellow stars and bright white stars. I look away giving time for my night vision to kick back in. The gen up top providing power below has cut out. It is eerily peaceful in the pit without the mono rope running or digging or air pumping out of the duct into the pit. Everyone is standing around adjusting to the dim light. I'm told this is another regular occurrence. Either it's a breakdown or the gen has run out of fuel – again. The work carries on, relying on lamp light and torches, making it an opportune time for the miners to steal yet more Tanzanite.

"Mate, how long is the gen off for, normally?" I enquire of Colin.

"Should be back on in five or so – probably just run out of fuel."

I am reassured. Ten minutes go by, fifteen and then thirty. It's getting very close and humid and the miners have stopped work – too hard to work sucking in what little air was left. *So, this is what it's like to be buried alive.*

"Okay, if it's not back on in another five, we're out of here," Colin instructs me.

"So how long would we have down here, mate, before we need to leave?" I ask.

"Maybe ten minutes; not much longer," is his reply.

This is my first venture underground. I have experienced a rock fall and near suffocation. Suddenly the flood lights burst to life. *You bloody beauty*, the gen is back on and with that the air ducting vent spews out soiled air, filling the chamber with a rusty-brown fog. *What! Now they want to gas us too?* It is the ducting clearing itself of the muck that has settled during the power outage. No wonder the air tastes like shit; and I'm sucking that into my lungs.

Pulling my t-shirt up over my mouth and nose, I try to filter the air. The miners have done the same, pulling up the cloth tied around their necks and proceed to use it for this exact same purpose. A well-practised procedure it would appear. What I hadn't noticed during the darkness was the ground water level rising.

Of course! No power to pump the water out! I am left wondering the many ways we can die. Suffocation, drowning or crushed to death. Okay, enough for my first baptism of underground mining in Tanzania, one of many to come, and not one was enjoyable.

Back at the office, Chris tells me how they have tried to chase the Jangali out of the shafts. The Jangali started throwing IEDs

(Improvised Explosive Devices) at them, plastic water bottles filled with dirt and a detonator shoved in the top. *Crude, but effective.* A detonator going off in your hand will take your fingers off. Add shrapnel and you get a fragmentation grenade. In response, the expats upped the ante and took shotguns with them into the shafts. Things got nasty when sticks of power gel were then added to the IEDs. More concerning was that the explosives were stolen from the mine's own explosives magazine.

In the ensuing weeks and months, I visit the sorting room, lapidary, machine shops, accompany Chris with shipments of Tanzanite into Arusha and visit the show rooms and sales office. Together we uncover a credit card fraud racket run by sales staff which turned out to be the largest Barclays credit card fraud case in Tanzania at the time.

I mentioned that the Askari carried shotguns down in the shafts. I do a weapons inspection and find the majority to be in shit condition. At least half of the weapons were fucked. Broken, missing parts or just simply seized up with rust. Some of the Askari carry them unloaded. Others had improvised slings (made from rope or electrical wire) which rendered the pump action inoperable. They have this mentality that if they carry a shotgun, they are important, at least in the eyes of their fellow countrymen. Doesn't really matter I guess, as it is obvious, they aren't prepared to use them on the Jangali anyway.

Between all this and a lack of accountability, there is a distinct disconnect between management, operations and security. Each department just gets on with their lot and what the others do is not their problem. There is obvious frustration amongst the expats. Chris had his arse hanging out but with a new ally, he was revelling in having time to do the job he was originally hired for.

After much discussion with Chris and the mine manager, Wes, another Jarpy, we set out to disrupt the illegal activities above and below ground. I make new procedures:

Gurkhas placed in areas identified with high exposure of Tanzanite, and the Askari re-assigned and given less responsibility and thus less opportunity to conspire with the Jangali.

Regular and random patrols of the mining lease.

Daily submission of duty reports through the chain of command for accountability

More lighting at the mine-face…

And new policies:

All mobile phones are to be left at the gatehouse on entry

Employees to wear IDs

Random searches above and below ground.

No plastic food wrapping to be taken underground, and so it went.

We really needed another contingent of Gurkhas to effectively cover the roles previously performed by the Askari.

The Gurkhas we have are working twelve, fourteen plus hour days, seven days a week as it is. This is going to prove a hard one and the government steps in, citing hiring of local labour in preference to third-country nationals, and some other bullshit local labour laws, it is obvious someone is getting a kickback from the brokers and jewellers.

Trying to sack a local proved impossible, even when caught red-handed stealing. A tribunal system that made a mockery of any resemblance of a judicial system and presided over by a fellow-worker from the same village as the accused. No one ever gets found guilty or sacked. You don't have to be a rocket scientist to work out why! I try to get an x-ray machine re-commissioned, but some wanker reckons that the radiation emitted from the machine is dangerous. Bullshit, the issue is that it works and will catch the thieving bastards with the stones shoved up their arse. That strategy is pushed to the backburner, but not forgotten, I will just have to re-think my strategy for its reintroduction.

What I am doing isn't anything spectacular by any means, but it was at least upsetting the illegal trade in Tanzanite. Our strategies are working. Restricting the role of the Askari is also affecting the Jangali. They don't know which shaft will or won't be in operation and thereby are not able to pick a shaft that is producing. This results in seventeen Jangali being caught in a shaft in one day which proves very fruitful for intel, as one of them turns informant. He is able to confirm our suspicions and identify the key players. Of course, he is doing this to protect his own backside. No one rolls over for other than selfish reasons, a reality I had learnt while in the Police Witness Protection Unit.

Chris and I are able to start compiling an intel (Intelligence) portfolio on the illegal activities, who the Jangali work for, who the brokers are and put names to faces. We re-assign miners to work in different areas and effectively take them out of circulation. Those few honest Askari encouraged by our work start to take an active role and become useful members of the security team. We start to enjoy the fruits of our labour, but we are also starting to get feedback that the illegal gem brokers down to the Askari are getting seriously pissed off. We have upset their illegal operations.

Veiled threats are now being made. My work was far from done, *fucking love it when this craps starts. Bring it on*. Handing the seventeen Jangali over to the local police with an evidence brief already prepared for them is a pointless exercise. They are released within hours, with no charges. Of course, the Officer in Charge at the local village police station is likely to be some dick relative of the Jangali. *I'm a dumb prick, I should have seen that one coming.*

Now you can probably understand my hesitation at first to climb out of the ore cart I was stuck in halfway down the mine shaft.

I did get some downtime while in Tanzania. The company is a sponsor of the Mount Kilimanjaro Marathon which attracts amateurs and professional marathon runners alike from around the world. Halfway up the mountain, we run a refreshment stand for the competitors and Chris has entered himself into the race. With bunting advertising the mining company flapping in the wind, we have fresh water and sponges for the racegoers as they pass. For this we need to keep our own fluids up, of course, which is achieved with a plentiful supply of cold Kili beer. I am amazed by the African runners. They run up the mountain as fast as they run down it, not reaching out for a drink or wet sponge and wearing 'Dunlop Volley' runners, whereas the westerners sport the latest Asics Gel runners and moisture-wicking Nike singlets, grabbing a cup of water in one hand and a sponge in the other. Some stop to revive whilst others spill more than they swallow. Not that it did anything for their performance. Chris holds his own and finishes the race. A great achievement for him personally. Mind you, he couldn't walk for two days afterwards, the poor bastard. A good effort considering the difficulty he had training up for it.

As the day wore on, we get more pissed. Two girls from the Arusha sales office have joined us and are getting into the spirit of the day. Soon the wet sponges find their mark and it quickly turns into a wet t-shirt contest. Angelique is a French national, mid 20s and with a very tight figure under her three-quarter-length Fabergé jeans and t-shirt, Margaret, a local national Arusha girl with ample cleavage bouncing all over the place and a glorious smile. Both girls are cleared during our investigation of the fraud scam in Arusha and the mine management has invited them along to show their appreciation for their loyalty and assistance in our investigation.

The girls are loving the cold water and ice cooling them off. At 900m above sea level, the Tanzanian sun still has a bite in it. All the crew are enjoying the impromptu entertainment, even if the girls don't know it. The night drive back to the mine is hilarious. Bouncing around in the back of utes, drinking cold Kili and stopping for leaks by the side of the road. We are all covered in dust and have sore arses from bouncing up and down in the back of the utes. From time to time, an arm reaches out through a passenger window and another couple of Kili are passed over. It is the perfect opportunity to get the Gurkha guard involved, away from the mine, and show them our appreciation for their hard work. They evidently have enjoyed their day's outing, having a laugh and a few beers, relaxing and getting to know everyone that little bit better.

My last day at the mine is an eventful one. Not since Iraq did I feel the need to sleep with a gun under my pillow. One of our trusted Askari has caught a Jangali coming out of a hole on the lease, the Jangali's head popping up out of the ground like a Meerkat. Buoyed by his capture, the Askari commences to frog-march him back to the security office only to be confronted by a group of marauding Jangali crossing the fence-line from one of the villages. Threats are exchanged and the Jangali try to overpower him and gain the release of his captive. The Askari lets rip with a few rounds from the shotgun and the hordes back off. In hindsight, probably not the best move but at least he took action, action that he and a few others had not been previously willing or supported to take. This stirs up all the Jangali and they mass on the fence line. Word soon filters back that they are threatening to cross en-masse and destroy whatever they can. Chris informs me that a few years back they did actually do something similar, torching a couple of the mill houses and stealing whatever was of value or use to them. It caused the closure of the mine.

Chris and a couple of the Jarpy's and myself head down for a look-see. Well fuck me, it was like a scene from Zulu Dawn – no pun intended. Standing along the non-existent fence-line there must be hundreds of Jangali, probably close to 500. They are yelling in their native Swahili what I can only assume are threats and abuse and the waving of machetes, with the odd "bomb" hurled in our general direction for good measure. Dusk is falling. Night-time is when they are most likely to attack. Okay, we we're well outside the effective range of the IEDs. But we can't discount the possibility that one of them, or more, may be armed with an AK.

Henny gets a call on the radio that the cavalry has arrived. *Thank fuck,* I think, only to be disappointed when two local coppers rock up. You can tell by the look on their faces that they do not want to be here. One is armed with an AK and the other with a 40mm grenade launcher. Fuck knows what he had in it, if in fact it is even loaded. They stay for five minutes and leave. *Fuck you very much,* I think. Okay, now we know we are on our own as far as backup from the police goes. We decide to re-group back at the office and assess our options.

Fortuitously, in the weeks prior, I had drafted an emergency evac plan for this exact kind of event. With regard to neighbouring states, we'd have a long haul to get to what we might consider a 'friendly' nation. We kick-start my plan of action, calling mine management to muster and start preparations. Vehicles, food and water, medical kits, comms, maps, Go Bags and so on. Everything should be ready to go within one hour. As for weapons, we have a couple of 9-mm FN (Fabrique Nationale) pistols, and a couple of 5.56mm bolt-action rifles. All functioning shotguns are underground with the Gurkhas. We are limited to one full mag for each of the pistols and limited rounds for the rifles. We're not supposed to have any of these weapons but as they were deemed necessary after the first skirmish, someone had 'acquired' them. Now I reckon I'm a fair shot with a pistol and could get a whole mag off, dropping a half dozen or so before being overrun, but it won't be enough. Not the most comforting of thoughts. We decide we need to keep a visible presence, a show of our supposed strength. Between five of us we take turns driving the 4wd's, trail bikes and moving around on foot, flashing our vast armoury of weapons for all the Jangali to see, giving an impression of a well-armed force. Worst-case scenario, this would allow time to get everyone above ground and finalise the arrangements of our evac. As the night progresses things start to calm down. Jangali numbers thin a bit and they are less vocal. Most likely because of working underground for the past week or more, hungry and they just really can't be fucked with it all anymore. They probably got pissed off with the smell of the Braai (BBQ) drifting across from our camp. The Jarpy's still put on a Braai as a send-off for me later that night.

I have made some more friends in another foreign land. But tonight, I keep a pistol under my pillow in case the Jangali get adventurous.

Jangali (Illegal Miners). Mill House No4
Faces obscured to protect the innocent

Jangali, entombed in a collapsed shaft

One of the villages surrounding the mining lease

Chapter 18

Frequent Flyers

I mentioned before that it's a small world, and yet again I found myself waiting in another airport terminal in Africa, this time Cote D 'Ivoire, and this time with a colleague I had worked with for that risk management company in Fremantle some four years back. We had both just finished a gig for my mate GT at OAM in Mali. I had started this gig in October 2016 through to the end of January 2017. It was supposed to recommence in mid-2017 but, as these contracts can often be influenced by other factors, it wasn't until November 2017 before I was to return, and now we are heading home once more in time for Christmas 2017.

For me personally, whilst from the training aspect I achieved what was required, the rest had been a bit of a train wreck. I had come down with Malaria in Bamako and I was recovering from that at the mine site when I managed to suffer a full tare of the supraspinatus in my left shoulder whilst teaching my students restraints, playing 'Crash Test Dummy' for them. But the job had to be done so I had put up with it until I could get home and sort it out. It required a full reconstruction job on the shoulder.

Killing time, sipping my drink of the moment, Vodka and Soda, we relax in the members lounge at the airport chatting about all manner of things when the subject of writing came up. Jon tells me he is writing a book about his time as an officer in Her Majesty's armed forces. Jon had also fallen victim to the failed Fremantle business and was now on the contracting circuit, be it at management level. He had been christened 'Lord Farquaad' from the movie 'Shrek' – not because of his looks or fiendish mind but because of his English upper schoolboy persona.

Jon is obviously officer type material, but by no means a 'Rupert' and probably why he did not complete Sandhurst or stay in Her Majesty's armed forces. Not only equipped with a wicked dry sense of humour, he is also a natural leader, able to back himself and he had earnt the respect of his charges, all of whom are former Australian, British, Fijian and NZ military.

As usual, we are having our morning brew standing around outside the site office and the banter goes back and forth at speed when someone compares Jon to Lord Farquaad, resulting in us all pissing ourselves; funny as fuck and so the name stuck.

I pass my laptop across to Lord Farquaad, opened on the first chapter of this, my book. Immediately he encourages me to add a chapter about my taxi ride across two West African states on my last visit to Mali that I had just related to him over our drinks. I explain how I wrote the book during my dad's battle with cancer and that the taxi ride was post-Dad's passing, but Jon in his eloquent and persuasive manner insisted I write the chapter. Here you go and thankyou Jon for suggesting I do.

Bamako Senou Airport, Mali. International Departures 2017 0730am.

In her best English, the ticketing girl takes my passport and checks it against the flight manifest.

"Mr Simmoon Grievous, we have confirmed Bamako to Lome on Asky. Lome to Accra cancelled" said in a very matter of fact way, almost blasé.

WTF. I look at my travel fixer, who looks at me, smiles and shrugs. I had given up on correcting the locals on the pronunciation of my name, I know who I am.

"Mr Simmoon, we will arrange a hotel for you in Lome and connecting flight." This is what she comes back at me with on seeing my pissed-off look. I should have guessed it was lip service.

I look at Olivier, my 'fixer'. "What do you think, Olivier?"

"I think this will be okay, Mr Simmoon." And gives the wide white teeth African smile that really says, 'I don't really know or care.'

Okay, I'm up for a few shits and giggles, never been to Togo, so why not?

After a relatively short flight from Mali to Togo, a small nation squashed between Ghana and Benin, and the stampede across the tarmac to grab your bags and be first through immigration, I find myself standing in the middle of the Arrivals hall looking for someone who knows what the fuck is going on. The minute anyone wearing a uniform saw me looking around to grab some help, they spin around on their heels and are gone. I manage to snaffle and unsuspecting employee, and bingo!

"Sir, please take a seat here. I will be back shortly to help you."

Ushering me to a row of plastic seats in the Arrivals hall, I take my seat full of optimism. *You beauty*, I think, *finally getting somewhere*. An hour later, I am still sitting in the Arrivals hall waiting for the phantom customer service officer to return. *More lip service*. This is bullshit and I'm off in search of someone in authority. Considering Togo is only a small nation, their airport is quite impressive; light and bright in design. I take a set of escalators up to nowhere in particular. I read on the glass door: ASKY MANAGERS OFFICE', KNOCK AND WALK IN.

In my best French, "Par Lay Vu Anglaise."

"Oi, missuer." A lady greets me with a warm smile and handshake.

I might actually get somewhere now, I am thinking.

Between broken English, poor French and hand gestures, I explain that I have been bounced off my flight from Lome to Accra and will miss my connecting flight to Dubai and home, Australia. Madame taps away on the computer, makes several phone calls, checking and re-checking my travel itinerary. She tells me that there is no record of any arrangements for a hotel overnight or connecting flight. I am not a happy camper, not only with Asky. My advice to anyone is: if you're ever in West Africa, never fly Asky. I am not happy with Olivier, my fixer, either for not following up on the arrangements from his end. I should have taken his supercilious look on his face as a warning and followed up myself.

Madame makes more calls and entries into her computer. "Mr Simmoon, I can get you on a flight to Beirut and connecting with Emirates to Dubai," she says with some anticipation of hope in her voice.

Beirut, Lebanon. Yeah, no, I don't think so. But I don't want to piss madame off as she is trying so hard for me, so I ask, "Are there any alternative routes?"

After more pondering on the computer and a few more phone calls, she comes back at me with a curve ball. "If you leave now, we will pay for a taxi to drive you to Accra."

Well, I didn't see that one coming. I enquire, "Okay, how long would that take?"

Madame replies with five or six hours if I leave straight away and I will still catch my connecting flight to Dubai. Asky will pay for the taxi.

Taxi. I'm thinking minibus, people mover, or an actual taxi. Oh, how wrong I am. Waiting outside the terminal at the pickup/drop off stand is a maroon coloured 1980 Mercedes that had definitely seen better days, and a driver who was obviously very happy to be picking up the fare. As it turns out, it's not actually a taxi, or at least not a *registered* taxi, just some guy Aksy have collared for a quick earn. So, with my suitcase unceremoniously dumped in the boot and me hanging onto my day bag, I jump in the back and we hit the road for Accra, Ghana – only around two hundred kilometres as the crow flies.

The driver spoke reasonable English but, given the air-con doesn't work and all the windows are open to get the air moving through the cab, conversation is difficult anyway. It is doing nothing to battle the sweat that is now starting to soak my t-shirt, sitting back against the vinyl bench seat. I am thankful for grabbing a litre bottle of water before leaving the airport, although the chill had long since left it.

Digging my mobile out of my day pack, I check … *no signal, bugger. Should have made few calls before I left the airport. I'll worry about all that when I get to Accra.* Tommi Makinen, the driver in East Kalimantan had nothing on this guy. I quickly came to the conclusion that either he did not own the car, or he just didn't give a shit. We were hitting potholes without any effort to avoid them, overtaking lines of trucks on bends, on hills with the speedo hitting ninety miles per hour.

"Mate, you reckon we will make Accra before 5pm?"

(*Before we die!!*)

Smiling and looking over his shoulder he replies, "Yes, yes … I know these roads very well, we will make it," he reassures me. If he had said 'Inshallah' I reckon I would have smacked him in the back of the head. I was feeling, well, a little tense, let's just say.

Traffic was building both ways as we approach the border of Togo and Ghana. I look at my watch: 2.30pm. My water bottle is empty, and I had not eaten since about 5am. I am hot and sticky, but not in a good way. Playing a game of cat and mouse, for the next fifteen minutes we weave our way up the highway, darting in and out between lines of trucks and buses to avoid the oncoming traffic. We had travelled pretty much parallel to the coast and now as we drew closer to the border crossing town of Aflao, traffic is just manic. Everything and everyone must pass through border control and we had stopped some five hundred metres short of the control point. My driver tells me we will have to walk to border control for a passport check.

Peeling myself off the seat separating vinyl from t-shirt and skin, I clamber across the seat and out of the taxi, grab my suitcase out of the boot, sling my day pack over my shoulder and, checking I have the important things in my jeans pockets – passport, vaccination card, wallet and mobile – *Bingo*. So, we set off walking through the stagnant cars, idling trucks and locals meandering between. My suitcase thankfully has rollers and a telescopic handle so I can pull it along, but the rough bitumen road is chewing the plastic rollers to pieces. *Was probably time I got a new suitcase anyway.* I wonder how this is going to work: we have left the taxi parked up to go to customs and immigration – do we then walk all the way back to the taxi and drive through? Didn't make sense to me, but then again, the way Africans do a lot of things doesn't make sense.

The highway is controlled by a boom gate dropped across it with turnstile gates for pedestrians to negotiate once clearing border control. Trucks are allowed to pass once ID and manifests are checked and the boom gate is lifted. Stepping up into a green and yellow painted concrete room with a wooden topped counter running from the doorway to another office, Immigration is the first stop and is the office adjacent to Customs. Everyone of any official capacity is in paramilitary uniform of some sort, some with gold or red lanyards over their shoulder contrasting with the dark green of the uniform. Handing my yellow vaccinations card to the officer behind the counter, my driver rattles off to him in French.

"Yellow Fever?" quizzes the Immigration officer, who bears a remarkable resemblance to Idi Amen.

I point to the date and signature next to the immigration stamp when I first arrived in Ghana.

Dada Amen dismisses my response. "This is not current."

I go on to explain that the yellow fever vaccination is now valid for life, not ten years as it used to be. His argument is that the date of my last jab in 2014 preceded that ruling and therefore was not valid. My reasoning is that I was allowed to enter Ghana and onward travel to Mali and now I cannot leave. Surely if I was a risk, they would not let me into Ghana or Mali in the first place on the very same document?

He informs me he is an expert in immunisation and has just returned from a World Health Organisation conference about yellow fever blah, blah, blah. I counter with the date still fell within the ten years postdate vaccination. Then the clincher: wouldn't you know it ... to resolve this 'problem' I would have to pay the fee for a yellow fever vaccination. I am just another opportunity to make a buck out of some unsuspecting westerner who is perceived to have lots of money. I understand it, and admire anyone who shows some entrepreneurial skills, but be smart how you go about it and select your target customer, and this time he has fucked up. I argue the point and tell him I only have a small amount of 'CFA' (African Franc) currency and no Ghanaian cedi. Idi Amen seems to concede that he is not going to get any money out of me and, on this occasion, has picked the wrong mark. Waved off, I move into the Customs office, dragging my suit case to be greeted by another uniformed official but somewhat more friendly. "Please take a seat."

I hand over my passport and vaccination card and he duly stamps my Ghana visa page in my passport, hands it back and I am on my way.

Well, bugger me, that was easy. Easier than trying to get through the turnstile with my bloody suitcase and day pack. They don't make these things for westerners, that's for sure, or at least not of my build, as I turn sideways, manoeuvring the day pack onto my left shoulder and dragging my suitcase sideways, which really didn't do the roller wheels any good. To my pleasant surprise, upon exiting out the other side, I am not swamped by 'porters' offering to carry my bags. My driver points me toward a walkway opening into a small gravel carpark at the rear where his Mercedes is parked and waiting. The Africans do really work in mysterious ways.

And here we go again, hitting the highway at ninety kilometres an hour and looking at my watch. I didn't realise we had lost a good hour at border control, thanks to Idi Amen. It was now 4pm.

The traffic gradually thinning as we make distance on Togo, racing through Ghana, passing villages lining the highway and lush greenery between. The heat is still stifling in the late afternoon. I had gone past the point of being hungry now, but my mouth was as dry as a nun's cunt. My flight was due to depart at 5.30pm, we had an hour left to get there. It was going to be a tight one and I found myself constantly glancing at my watch. It kept my mind off Evil Knievel's driving anyway.

It's not long before we hit traffic again as villages turn into towns on the outer suburbs of Accra, and peak hour traffic. I lean forward to speak with Evil Knievel.

"We going to make it on time?"

His over-confident reply does nothing to reassure me. "I drive this road many, many times, we will make it."

Ah shit! Now traffic control lights, which do absolutely no good whatsoever to 'control' the traffic! An oxymoron I think they call it when drivers ignore the signals or decide that they are in the wrong lane and try to change lanes midstream. We've slowed to twenty kilometres an hour, which was a pleasant change from the white-knuckle ride through Togo, but in doing so has slowed our progress to the airport. I can see the airport in the distance, planes landing, taking off and the flashing beacon of the airport control tower.

Another glance at my watch: 4.30pm. Now I am working on the theory that flights in Africa are notorious for being late, both on arrival and departure, which should buy me some leeway. But I find myself leaning forward against the front seat and looking at my watch again. In the next ten minutes we manage to move maybe a kilometre, only adding to my frustration as we near the peripheries of the airport boundary. 4.45pm. Fuck, another set of lights, and up ahead and about another 500 metres further on, I can see the turn off to the airport terminal.

"I'll run from here, mate, or I will never make it."

With that, I was up and out before Evil Knievel had time to answer. Tapping on the boot, he pops the lid and I grab my suitcase. Rather than try pulling it, I grab the carry handle and hoof it down the road between the line of traffic. Changing hands, I am working up a sweat big time in the stifling humidity. Turning up the road to International Departures, the legs are working overtime and I am swapping hands more frequently as my suitcase takes on more weight. I continue swapping hands as my left shoulder gives out. Stepping up onto the footpath, I put the suitcase down and decide to pull it regardless of what state the rollers are in, as I try to run up the incline to the International Terminal. My shirt is plastered to my skin, wet through from sweat. Even my jeans feel damp. Getting through security and into the terminal, I start the hunt for the Emirates counter. 5.15pm. I spot an Emirates worker walking through the terminal.

"Excuse me, excuse me, please. Where's the Emirates check in?"

Her answer was not what I wanted to hear. "I'm sorry, they are closed, and the flight has boarded."

I think she sensed my frustration as I had that look like many get when they have missed their flight. "You'll have to come back at 11.30 in the morning and we'll see what we can do about getting you on another flight. There's no more flights tonight."

Fuck it, what to do next? Frustrated, hot, tired and thirsty, I decided I need a base to operate from and get my shit together and start making phone calls. It costs me twenty US dollars to get a taxi from the airport to the Ibis Style hotel, which in reality I could have walked but was just too shagged.

Longing for air-conditioning and a long cold beer, I enter reception of the Ibis Style hotel. Not the most luxurious of hotels but for a hotel chain it is comfortable, clean and not too badly priced at US$270 a night. Handing over my passport, the receptionist steps back from the counter, which I thought was a bit odd but thought nothing more about it.

"Mr Grievous, we do not have a reservation for you?"

I explained, told her I am paying on Visa and she hands over the key card to my room.

Walking past the bar on my way to the lifts, I check out the selection of tap beers, thinking I will be having a few cold ones very shortly. Swiping the card over the reader, I enter my room, throw my day pack on the bed and push the suitcase into a corner out the way. Then my nostrils are violently assaulted. *What is that smell? There's a dead body in my room! No, hang on, it's me. I fucking stink.* Then it dawned on me, that's why the girl at reception took a step back when I booked in. I'm on the nose big time. Six weeks of eating local food, some twelve hours since my last shower, sweating like a pig in a taxi all day, plus the run up to the airport, it's oozing out of my skin. *Shower, now, then beer.*

Feeling for the most part human again after a good long shower and scrub, I head to the bar for a few take-aways before phoning home. A little more relaxed after downing the first beer, I fire up the laptop and bang off an email to the boss and brief him of what has transpired. Next, I call my wife and let her know I am in Ghana, explaining how I got bumped off the flight in Togo.

"Soooo, how did you get to Accra if you missed your flight?"

Ah yeah, she's got me on that one. Silence, I didn't answer.

"You didn't drive, did you?"

What else can I say?

"I might not have."

Am I going to get an ear bashing when I get home, but justly deserved, I guess? I calm her down, reassuring her the taxi was fine, explaining I would have called but needed to get on the road straight away and there is no phone reception out in the middle of butt fuck nowhere West Africa. I don't think she bought it, she's a bit smarter than that.

Next, flights. I need to get a flight home. Given the time difference it worked out quite well being daytime back in Perth, the wife started the call around, to OAM, the corporate travel agent and Emirates. So went the night, between calls back and forth, grabbing an hour's kip and checking email updates. Around midnight Ghana-time, we had managed to get on the same Emirates flight I was supposed to catch, only a day late. Better still, an 11.30am flight out so a bit of a sleep in. *You beauty*. But first, that stinking shirt has to go in the rubbish. It had been irritating my nostrils since I had binned it after my shower. I stuck my head out the door, looked up and down the corridor and promptly dumped the shirt in a bin next to an ice machine.

Illegal miners digging into the step walls of the open cut, stopping excavation operations, endangering their own lives.
Many are from Bakina Faso and their numbers rapidly grow.
ASM is funding terrorism across the Sahel.

QRF Team Vehicle Deployment

My first tour of Mali. Fijian students.

End of Tour windup. A few drinks and a game of pool and relaxing with my Fijian colleagues

2nd tour to Bamako. My Malian student cohort who I would train and travel to site for continuation training and deployment

Gateway to Mali capital, Bamako

Typical street scene around the capital

Chapter 19

Blue Blood

There's an old saying: Once a cop always a cop. And it is true. The blood that runs through my veins is blue. I will always bleed blue and I will always support the Thin Blue Line. Of course, I do not support or condone the actions of all Police – there are rotten apples in every job but in the most part they are weeded out. If anything, I think we, as coppers, tend to be harder on our own, evident that we are not afforded the presumption of innocence as are the guilty until proven otherwise.

As I said at the start, I am nothing special. I'm not a hero and I am not looking for accolades, I made mistakes. There are, however, Police Officers past and present that do deserve recognition for going way, way beyond the Call of Duty. I have bled blue for the job and for the people I swore to protect, and I accept that. Would I do it again? Probably. Would I change anything I did back then? No, it is who I am, and it has helped make me who I am today.

What I have hopefully achieved by writing this book is to demonstrate that Police are normal everyday people who live amongst you. On the most part, you will most likely never get to know us unless you are a victim or a criminal, and on our part, we hope to have never meet you either way. We are normal people who have put our hand up to do an increasingly difficult job. You have the opportunity or choice to join and chose not to.

The very fabric of our society is the result of our own doing and I can't help but feel we are in the predicament we are today because of what and whom, as a society, we have listened to. When I first started dating my now wife, she didn't understand my own, or my copper mate's, black humour. Over time, she came to experience and understand my frustration, sadness, joy, anger and all the other range of emotions that come with being a Police Officer. She was also to learn the truth, from me, not what the pollies or the journos and keyboard warriors who espouse their narrative to suit whatever agenda. She understands, now, our black humour is a coping mechanism to doing the job.

> **THE POLICE OFFICER**
>
> Of all men and women in society you are the most needed,
> yet least welcome on the doorstep.
> A strange namelsss creature
> who is 'hero' to some, and 'filth' to others.
> You are such a diplomat that you can settle an argument
> leaving both sides thinking that they've won.
> If you look smart, you're arrogant.
> If you're untidy, you're a disgrace.
> You must make instant decisions that
> would take lawyers months to sort out.
> You must be the first at an accident
> and remain in complete control.
> You must start breathing and stop bleeding,
> Accept all complaints with absolute charm.
> You must be able to restrain a man twice your size
> without being brutal.
> If he hits you you're a coward.
> If you hit him you're a bully.
> You're expected to hold down a drunk with one hand,
> and rescue a cat with the other.
> Hunt down the drug pusher and comfort the bereaved
> as a matter of daily routine.
> No wonder that only one person in four hundred is a Police Officer!

Author unknown

www.ingramcontent.com/pod-product-compliance
Lightning Source LLC
Chambersburg PA
CBHW070353120526
44590CB00014B/1124